D1082156

Far Away Islands of Paradise

Also by LeCain W. Smith

Sailing South 'til the Butter Melts

Our Inner Ocean: A World of Healthy Modalities

A Maritime History of Brooksville, Maine

Steel Away: A Guidebook to the World of Steel Sailboats

Far Away Islands of Paradise

The second book in the series

The Amazing Adventures of the Sea Cat Chowder

As told to the author

LeCain W. Smith

by the Sea Cat Chowder

Windrose Productions
Harborside, ME

Windrose Productions
997 Cape Rosier Road
Harborside, ME 04642

www.WindroseAway.com

ISBN 978-0-9615508-6-8

Printed in the United States of America

Illustrations by LeCain W. Smith and Jim Kosinski

To the awesome Pacific islanders,
who invited us into their homes and
took us into their hearts

Contents

 # Acknowledgements

First and foremost, I must thank my precious feline companion Chowder. Without her loving input, this book would not have been created. Next, I give great appreciation for my primary proof reader, editor, and advisor Sheila Moir, who also created the layout of this book. In addition, my thanks to Martha Jordan, and Elaine Hewes for their proofreading and suggestions. The feedback from a number of children who read the manuscript is also greatly appreciated. As for the images, many thanks to artists Annie Poole and Gail Page for their analysis and comments. Last but not least, my deepest gratitude to digital wizard Jim Kosinski for his creation of the cover and back cover and for his invaluable, endless help in the final modification of all my interior drawings.

Introduction

Hello again! It's Chowder the global puss cat speaking. Welcome to the second book in the trilogy about my true-life adventures cruising around the world for six years on a forty-four-foot sailboat with my captain Lee, first mate Sheila, and some occasional extra crew.

In the first book, I talked about my early days living on land, some background about what the cruising life is like, a few stories about other notable sea cats, how my life at sea started, and my initial days of sea training. I continued with the first part of our global voyage as we sailed down the west coast of the U.S.A. to San Diego, California and beyond, with coastal cruising through Central America to Ecuador and the Galapagos Islands. This first part of the voyage lasted almost two years and was where I first got my sea legs. My paws have never been the same since.

Now we will continue from the Galapagos Islands across the South Pacific to various Polynesian islands of paradise. This part of the voyage primarily follows what is called the "milk run," where the trade winds blow and coconut trees grow. After over a year in these tropical waters, our voyage continues as we journey down under (further south) to New Zealand and then venture back up to Fiji and Vanuatu in the area of the western Pacific known as Melanesia. In the last part of this book, we sail north across the equator to the islands of Micronesia in the North Pacific Ocean

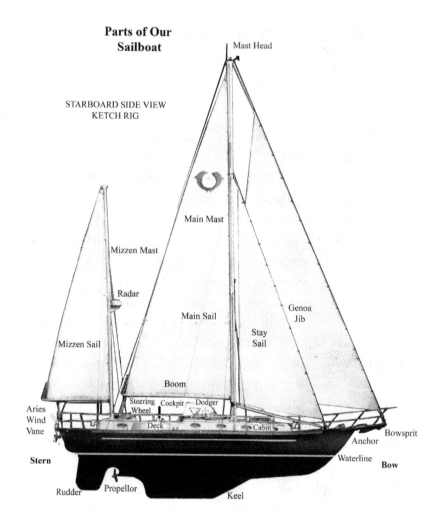

**Parts of Our
Sailboat**

STARBOARD SIDE VIEW
KETCH RIG

Mast Head

Main Mast

Mizzen Mast

Radar

Genoa
Jib

Main Sail

Stay
Sail

Mizzen Sail

Boom

Steering   Cockpit   Dodger
Wheel

Aries
Wind
Vane

Deck   Cabin   Bowsprit

Anchor

Stern   Waterline   Bow

Rudder   Propellor   Keel

and then cruise back south through the Solomon Sea to Papua New Guinea and across the Coral Sea to Australia, a place we call the Land of Oz. Plenty of amazing adventures to purr about!

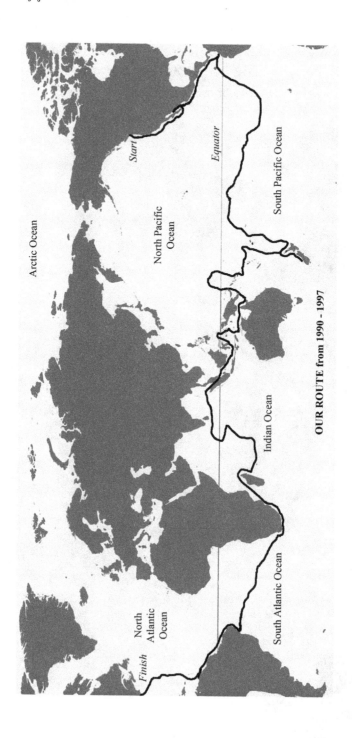

OUR ROUTE from 1990 - 1997

PART 1

Cruising with
the Trade Winds

CHAPTER 1
My First Long Ocean Crossing

Before I continue with our adventures across the Pacific Ocean, I would like to say something about life at sea. First, you should keep in mind that the cruising life is very different from life on land. It initially requires you to learn about seamanship and boat handling. Next, you need to have a good boat and crew, and you should get to know them well through day trips and short coastal hops. After you gain confidence and learn the basics of navigation, it is then time to venture beyond the horizon.

Long-distance global cruising is the ultimate in sea-life adventures. You will surely experience exciting times while encountering all the diversity that the world can offer. When at the mercy of the elements with changing weather and sea conditions, you have to adapt to constant changes and learn as you go through each experience. When exploring the world by sea, the reward is visiting many remote and exotic places with interesting people that would not be accessible by airplane.

Even though this lifestyle may not be for someone who prefers the security of living on land, many people or cats, if so inclined, can come to enjoy all the excitement and variety of experiences it offers. However, you need to realize that conditions during an ocean voyage are in a constant state of change. Each sea crossing is different—some go smoothly with fine days of sailing in comfort, while others are rough and bouncy. A lot depends on the weather, the season, and what part of the world you are in. Of course, if you are brave and have salt in your veins, then you could take it all in stride. However, for a cat like me, I doubt that there is any salt in my veins. It took me a while to adapt to the lively motion of the rolling seas when conditions were rough. But over time, I did learn how to sway my body with the motion of the boat while sitting or walking.

Now we will return to our story with the departure from the Galapagos Islands. This time, we would be at sea for a much longer time, for we would cover a distance of around 1,970 miles before reaching the very remote and legendary place known as Easter Island. It was time for me to really become an able-bodied sea cat and learn about the challenges of cruising over long distances on the ocean.

At the end of Book One, upon our arrival in the Galapagos Islands, we were informed by the port captain that we could not stay more than ten hours since we didn't have the proper official entry forms. Captain Lee, first mate Sheila, and our temporary Argentinian crew member Elena were all disappointed about not being able to stay longer. But after sailing for a day through the islands to the southwest, we got used to the situation, and with our eyes on new horizons, we soon accepted things as they were. This was my first lesson in adapting to change. We knew more exciting times lay ahead of us, especially since our next destination was Easter Island.

Captain Lee was by now very confident in the capabilities of our boat, and Sheila had gained plenty of boat-handling experience during the initial part of our voyage down the west coast of the Americas. As for me, I admit to having more trust in both of them, and after almost two years of sailing, I felt very much at home on the boat. Even though I had some apprehension about a long ocean crossing, I had a feeling that all would be fine, just as long as I wasn't catapulted off the boat in rough seas!

It was a fine day when we sailed off from the Galapagos, and by that afternoon, we could no longer see land. I snuggled up under the dodger on my favorite pile of rope. It was a good place to watch the crew. Lee and Sheila, along with our new mate Elena who had joined us in Panama, took turns steering since the light winds made the self-steering device useless.

For the first few days, sea conditions were smooth with only a gentle swell from the south. We were still in the convergence zone close to the equator, where winds are usually light and variable. We would need to get further south in latitude before we reached the stronger prevailing trade winds that blew from the southeast. For now, the sun was shining, and we were free from bad weather.

I am happy to say that Lee caught a nice tuna fish during this time. I tried to help him, but my paws could not hold onto the fishing line. The tuna put up a good fight, and Lee had to struggle for a while to bring him in. When the fish was finally landed on deck, I stretched my claws in anticipation of a delightful meal full of tasty tidbits.

It was not long before steady trade winds arrived. At first, they were light winds that Lee called "baby trades." But they were strong enough that the Aries self-steering device could now be hooked up, thereby relieving the crew of the constant duty of steering the boat. Everyone could spend more time reading, relaxing, cooking meals, or sleeping. Lee always said that the crew is happier when they are more relaxed. I definitely agree with that. Still, they each had to take turns sharing the duty of staying topside and standing watch. This is a necessary rule of the sea that Lee strongly adhered to. No, you do not have to stand up,

but simply stay on deck and keep an eye for any passing ship or changes in sea or wind conditions.

I have often been asked what sailors do with the boat at sea during the night. You don't put an anchor out in the middle of the ocean, for the bottom of the sea is too far below. The twenty-four hours of each day at sea are divided into shifts, when each of the crew takes turns being in charge of standing watch and controlling where the boat is heading. During daytime, the shifts are more relaxed, while at night they are tightly structured. When there are only two sailors onboard, watches are divided into four-hour shifts, with some overlap for the new person to wake up, have some coffee, and get ready to take over. The mate who is about to retire can relay any pertinent information to the one coming on watch before they go below to sleep.

When there are more than two crew members, the length of a shift can be shortened, thereby making it easier for all involved. Some rough crossings can be quite tiresome with only two crew members on the boat, but if the self-steering device is doing its job, it is not so bad. Sailors standing watch during the last hour of their night shift may get very tired, so it may sometimes be necessary to wake another mate up earlier. No shame in that. There is always some flexibility in the timing. As for me, I could come and go and sleep when I felt like it.

For the human crew, standing watch on the first few days of a crossing is the hardest, because it often takes some time to adapt your sleeping patterns to this schedule. However, once you get into the rhythm, it becomes easier. In fact, it can be quite enjoyable to be on watch in the middle of the ocean with all the stars and the moon shining down from above. Sheila and Lee both had a special appreciation for the dawn shift and the early light of sunrise. As a cat, I like to be up at night and often had the duty of comforting whoever was on watch during the final hours of their shift. My keeping that mate company helped them stay awake. I also have good night vision and the ability to hear unusual distant sounds. If need be, I could sound an alarm with a long, deep meow. However, the crew was not always sure what that meant.

As time passed, my four legs got used to the motion of the boat, which was still not so bad and quite steady. But as Lee predicted, stronger trade winds soon came as we sailed further south. I now felt more secure when staying down below, for the boat was starting to heel over more while sailing close to the wind. I found that when lounging on the bunk on the lee side (the lower side of the boat when it heels over), I was secure, whether I was just resting or sleeping. Another spot on a high shelf made it easy for me to sit up and look out a porthole to see some sea birds diving for fish or get a good view of a nice sunset. I felt happy to be a sea cat.

To my astonishment, I must admit that before long, I found new sensations that were quite enjoyable. I began to love the rhythmic motion of the boat as it plowed along at a steady pace while prancing over the seas. This was especially true when the wave patterns were constant, because they tended to lull me to sleep while I rested down below. I would often get hypnotized by the sound of the water rushing by when I lay on the bunk up in the bow of the boat. It's like the sea was purring as the water rushed by just inches away on the outside of the hull. This provided a very soothing and wonderful feeling. I think Lee felt the same, for he often joined me there.

As the days passed to the constant rhythm of the rolling sea, each of the crew took turns sleeping, eating, and standing watch. At certain times, the trade winds would get stronger. Lee called them "reinforced trades." Trade winds normally blow between 12 and 24 knots (one knot equals 1.15 miles per hour), but when reinforced, they could blow up to around 35 knots. Since our course put us on a beam reach, where we were sailing at a right angle to the wind, the boat could easily handle it. We kept all the sails up and moved at a fast pace, covering many miles each day, which definitely helped reduce the duration of our passage. We were not racing, just moving faster. Lee was proud of the boat's performance. However, more wind changes the height and motion of the waves, and as the boat bounced along, it was harder to move about. The crew moved more slowly and carefully, making sure they had something to hold onto. I mostly stayed put in my cozy spots. For the moment, things were lively but basically good. I was adapting and starting to feel more comfortable as the days passed by.

For the most part, our long ocean crossing went well. Although the trade winds sometimes shifted in direction, we could still make sail adjustments and keep heading close to the rhumb line. A rhumb line is the most direct heading to a destination, and when we can head that way while keeping the boat on a beam

reach, all goes well. When the winds did shift more to the south, it became harder to hold our course. During this time, the boat bounced and plunged excessively as we headed closer into the waves. I had to developed new ways to keep myself stable and securely wedged in while snuggled in my bunk as the boat pranced along. I was glad that after a few days the winds shifted back to the southeast, making things easier.

There is one other thing that I will say about sea conditions. When sailing on the ocean, there really are two things that affect comfort and performance. Although the strength of wind is important, it is the condition of the sea that determines how well the boat moves along and how comfortable the crew is. First, there are the larger ocean swells that a sailboat can usually ride over easily. Then there are the waves that come on top of the swells. Depending on the winds and their direction, these waves can make the ride bouncy, especially when sailing into or across the trade winds. Sometimes they even splash into or over the boat.

All winds around the world pulsate and vary in strength, but the trade winds here in the tropics are the most constant in strength and direction. Still, a boat does best when sailing with the waves and winds behind her rather than when beating close-hauled into them. I had to learn all this, and now that you too have this basic information, let us return to the journey.

Each day at sea went by quickly, and we were getting closer to our destination. We did have an incident of equipment failure when sailing in the reinforced trades. One of the fittings connected to a line that holds the mainsail boom in place broke apart. This created a dangerous situation, because the boom could now swing around wildly without lines to control it. Anyone onboard could be hit in the head by the boom as it was flung about by the bouncy motion of the boat. The mainsail could also get torn if it hit the rigging wires. Lee and the crew had to quickly scramble to make the proper repairs. I am happy to say that they were successful in fixing the problem without any of us getting hurt.

As we got closer to Easter Island, the winds became lighter and more variable, since we were now moving out of the trade-wind zone into the mid-ocean area of the doldrums, the calmer center in the middle of every ocean around which stronger winds blow. Still, conditions were good enough to keep moving, and before long we came close to the island. Since it looked like we might arrive during the night, we reduced sail in order to slow down and get to the island the next morning in daylight. It is always best to arrive at an unknown place in daylight.

When dawn did come, it was like magic to see the island looming directly ahead of us. It looked like a large animal sleeping on the water. After nearly seventeen days at sea, it was a delight to be close to a strange, new island so far from anywhere. I purred at the thought of curling my tail and resting my wobbly body when the boat was in still waters in a sheltered cove.

CHAPTER 2
Easter Island Adventures

After anchoring off the main village and making radio contact with the officials, a local pilot was sent out to guide us through a narrow passage into a small cove to secure the boat and get our official clearance. The island has only a few anchorages, but none are well protected, and they are only good during times when the seas are calm. The little cove known as Hanga Piko was where we would keep the boat for the duration of our stay. Since there were six other visiting yachts already there and space was limited, we had to tie all the boats together in a row with anchors out and lines ashore to hold us in place. This is called rafting up, and we did look like a raft of differently shaped logs. This worked out fine, at least for the first few weeks during our stay.

Easter Island is a very unique place located many sea miles from any other land. Even though it is now part of the country of Chile in South America, this fascinating island has a rich and mysterious history. In the distant past, it was settled by migrating Polynesian people, who built large statues called "moai" that were carved out of the local volcanic-rock quarries. Hundreds of these statues, which resemble human figures, were somehow moved to different locations around the island and erected in a standing position with each facing out to sea. It is a big mystery as to how this was done. Some of the locals still say it was magic, while others say they were either rolled on logs or walked upright while being guided by ropes. In any case, it was an amazing feat. It is

believed that their purpose was to give praise to the gods and protect the native people.

The original inhabitants were voyagers who came by sailing canoe from distant lands. The history of these indigenous people is full of mystery, with stories and legends about their traditional customs, ritual ceremonies, and spiritual life. Some believe that after many peaceful years, problems with a shortage of resources developed, and a major civil war occurred. This forced some of the inhabitants to hide in the numerous caves scattered around the island. In the end, the civil war caused the death of many people, and the population was almost completely decimated. When seafarers first came from other parts of the world, they found only a few hundred indigenous people still living there. Then whaling ships came and spread disease, which further reduced the population. These ships also took a number of natives away to work for them as slaves. Over the years since then, Chilean settlers from South America arrived and now outnumber the Polynesians.

So much is not known about this volcanic island that popped up in the middle of the ocean. Much of the island's history has been researched by explorers and written about in books, but much remains a mystery. We heard various stories including tales about a strange birdman cult, locals with either long or short ears, and women who painted their faces white. Lee and Sheila were anxious to check things out first hand. They spent many days traveling by jeep and on foot across all parts of the island. Besides stone ruins with unusual carved images, they found caves that still contained human bones and other ancient artifacts left behind from the distant past. Lee even spent one night camping alone in one of the volcanoes. He had to sleep on a rock as the brushy ground had too many bugs crawling around. At one of the quarries, Sheila got to stand on a fallen statue that was over thirty feet long. They both felt that a subtle spirit from the mystical past still pervades on the island.

Meanwhile, I pondered what a birdman cult would have been like. All I heard was that it was a competition between warriors who had to swim out to a small offshore island to gather bird eggs and make it back without breaking the eggs. The first one to return with an unbroken egg was the winner. Sounded odd to me, for I would rather catch the birds. It also made me wonder how the eggs tasted.

During this time, I mostly hung out on the boat, although I could now hop over onto the other cruising boats that were rafted close to us. Initially, there were a number of celebratory parties, and a local fisherman we befriended brought us gifts that included piles of the avocados that grew wild on the island. Sheila was very good at making friends with the local women, and she often invited them for tea and homemade cake. The young girls that came with them were quite fascinated with me, for there were few "gatos" (cats) on the island. Each of them wanted to hold me, and

in the end, I had to go along with it, as more than one girl held me at the same time. I have to admit, they were quite gentle and gave me lots of sweet hugs.

During our stay, we made many local friends, and all the cruisers had a great time. There was even a Hollywood movie being made about the history of the island. So while we were there, each day was full of different activities. However, after a few weeks of fun and games, a major event occurred that would drastically change things for all the sailors moored in the cove.

The cause came from far away. When a big storm occurs in the ocean, its effects can sometimes be felt for hundreds of miles. Strong winds can create big waves that can travel very far from the center of the storm, especially over the open sea when unobstructed by land. In this instance, there was a gale far south in the latitude of the "roaring forties" off Australia. Yes, winds often do roar in this part of the world. It definitely sounded like a location where I would not like to be.

The large ocean swells created by that gale traveled all the way to Easter Island. Out of the blue, on what was a nice, sunny day, the swells grew into enormous waves that crashed ashore. As these walls of water came through the narrow entrance of the cove, they created a strong surge that pushed the boats back and forth. The water rose high over the land and then receded far back out before the next wave repeated the process. We were all caught off guard and scrambled to make things secure as boats in the raft-up were flung about. I sat bewildered, not sure what to do. All I could do was just watch in amazement.

This lasted all day and into the night. During that time, the repeated strain on the dock lines that held the weight of the seven boats tied together caused lines and deck fittings to break. This kept the sailors busy jumping around making repairs. A lookout was posted and yelled a warning as each wave came in. The port captain came down on the pier in his jeep, but it was flooded

by a large surge of water, and he left. The local radio station announced that the yachts might need some help, and one strong local man swam out with a large, heavy line to help secure the boats to shore. Some people brought tires to use as fenders to prevent the boats from bumping each other. Later, some women came down and prayed for the seas to subside. During the night, the situation was quite wild, and hardly anyone on the boats, including me, got any sleep.

When dawn came, we were happy that the waves had finally subsided, and we were glad that the damage to boats was not worse. Still, it took a while to put things back in order. A number of cruisers had to spend that day diving for lost anchors, untangling lines, and making repairs, while I sat exhausted from shattered nerves and lack of sleep.

After things settled down, the sailors on the yachts decided they should give thanks to the locals for their help by hosting a party with a grand feast. They hired women to prepare local foods and a farmer to rustle up a cow and cook it. Everyone in the village was invited. This included the local fisherman and the town officials, who didn't usually sit down for a feast together. It turned out to be quite an event, although a fairly expensive one for the cruisers. There was lots of music, singing, and dancing late into the night. Since it was too wild for me, I stayed on the boat. However, I could still hear all the nearby noise, and some of my young girl friends did stop by to see how I was doing.

A week later, we decided it was time for us to move on. We had stayed for over a month and made many friends, but more islands further west were calling to us. After loading the boat with fresh produce and getting lots of hugs and kisses, as well as pats for me, we headed out on our next long crossing of about 1,200 miles to Pitcairn Island.

CHAPTER 3
Pitcairn and the Tuamotus

The crossing to Pitcairn took us due west and lasted about eight-and-a-half days. During the first six days, the wind was quite strong, and we covered over a thousand miles. With the wind directly behind us, we set the sails in what is called a "wing and wing" position. That is when each of the two large primary sails (the main and the jib) are set out on opposite sides of the boat. It makes for a fun ride, but is also quite rolly when the boat surfs down the face of each following wave. I often found my belly rolling from side to side as I lay in my bunk thinking about the wings of birds. Eventually, I found myself lulled to sleep by the constant motion.

The days passed quickly, and except for spotting a few sea birds and two dolphins, not much happened. During the last two days, the wind dropped, the seas smoothed out, and we had to use the motor for part of the time before our arrival at Pitcairn Island. I was glad that Captain Lee was a good navigator, for that island is so small that you could easily miss it if your calculations were just a bit off the mark.

Like Easter Island, Pitcairn also has a unique history. You may have already heard the famous story. During previous centuries, when the tall sailing ships crossed the world's oceans, there was a ship called the *Bounty*. The captain of this ship, Captain Bligh, was very hard on the crew, and none of them liked him.

In the end, tensions got so bad that there was a mutiny. The disgruntled crew took over the ship, set the captain adrift in a small boat, and sailed off in search of an island to live on. They eventually found Pitcairn Island. After running the ship aground, scuttling it (deliberately sinking the ship), taking their supplies, and moving ashore, the crew made the island their new home. A number of the crew's descendants, with surname like Christian and Young, still live there to this day, and Lee and Sheila got to meet them. They are now a part of New Zealand and speak good Queen's English, but they converse with each other in their mid-eighteenth-century English dialect. We couldn't understand a word of it, and I didn't have a chance to talk to any of the cats.

The island doesn't have any real harbors. So, if sea conditions are not calm, any boat that visits must "heave to" off shore. When that happens only one small sail is left up so that the boat can stay steady, moving slowly back and forth just off the island with at least one crew member onboard standing watch. Therefore, it was necessary that the crew take turns to each get a visit ashore. Transportation ashore was in the one and only local longboat. It had to make a tricky, carefully timed landing through the breaking waves in a very small inlet by a pier along the shore of what is called Bounty Bay. What skilled boatmen these islanders are! I watched with fascination from the boat.

The sixty-five or so local inhabitants were very friendly and loved to have visitors. They took Lee and Sheila on scooters up

to their small village in the center of the island and gave them a tour of the area. They also gave them some fresh apples they had gotten from the crew of a passing freighter who had come ashore to get their passports stamped. All our crew, except for me, also had their passports stamped. Traveling sea cats have never been given passports, as far as I know. Why that is, I am not sure. It definitely makes for a nice, rare souvenir, since very few visitors come to Pitcairn.

After our mate Elena got her turn to go ashore and Lee and Sheila took a nice ride on small local powerboat around the island, we decided to head on. The seas were now a bit too rough for comfort when heaving to, and the crew had visited just about everyone on the island. So we hoisted all the sails and headed for Rikitea on the French island of Mangareva, which lay about 450 miles further west. That was fine by me, for I was looking forward to the steady motion of the boat when she sails along. I had come to enjoy how the rolling seas can make my body sway and rock me to sleep. Sounds like I am a real sea cat now, but I was really thinking about getting to the calm lagoon waters that I heard existed there.

The winds on this crossing were fair, but since they often shifted direction, the passage was slow. With some unusual zig-zag changes in our course, it took us over four days to get there. I spent most of my time simply watching Sheila do the cooking or Lee constantly adjusting the set of the sails to meet the changes in wind. Still, time passed quickly, and the crossing was over before we knew it.

Although Mangareva Island has a good-sized mountain that makes it easily visible from a fair distance offshore, it is surrounded by a dangerously low outer reef that enclosed a shallow lagoon. This type of tropical island is called an "atoll," and we would encounter many more like it during the years to come.

When coming close to an island like this, it is necessary to approach slowly and cautiously in order to find the entrance through the outer coral reef. We definitely did not want to run aground. Though we had some charts of this area, it was still necessary, when getting close, to have someone climb the rope ladder tied into the rigging wire by the mast to get a better view. Lee would usually be the one to climb up and give steering orders to the person at the helm, while I looked into the clear, shallow waters to see the colorful coral heads as we passed close by them. As a good climber, I had considered joining Lee aloft, but knew I would have difficulty coming down the ladder. Instead, I decided to exercise my claws by playing with some loose rope on deck.

Once inside, we found plenty of places to anchor in the calm, clear, protected turquoise waters of the shallow lagoon. It was extremely beautiful and peaceful. When we later found a spot to anchor close to the only village, Lee and the crew went ashore to clear in with customs and immigration and explore the surroundings.

This small group of islands, known as the Iles Gambier, are famous for pearls, sponges, and great diving on coral reefs. While diving on one reef, Lee and Sheila did find a shell, but the pearl was missing. At the local village, they discovered a wonderful French bakery that had very tasty homemade croissants and bread. Lee often ate all of it before returning to the boat, so Sheila had to return and get more the next day. Lee definitely likes to eat baked goods. They later hiked around the island and met many friendly people. The French-speaking locals that came on our boat called me "pussi." One of the many different names I would get on this voyage.

After a short visit to another anchorage on the west side of the lagoon, we headed out into the wild blue yonder on our next crossing. Our plan was to visit the very remote Austral Islands to the southwest. However, after a few days at sea, we found the winds were not cooperating, so we changed course for the Tuamotus, which lay further to the northwest. This region of the Pacific has a large number of low-lying atolls or "motus" that do not have any high land in their centers. Navigating in and around these dangerous islands requires extreme caution in order not to run aground on a reef. Therefore, it was essential to arrive in daylight, especially with the sun high overhead for the best view of the entrance. The electronic GPS device served us well, and after five days, we came to a small atoll called Motu Tunga.

When we entered the pass into the lagoon of this motu, we found that it was only a cul de sac that abruptly ended with a shallow inner reef. We could not get into a more protected location beyond the entrance. While we were considering the possibility of anchoring there, a man onshore waved to us. He said we could tie up along the wharf on the side of the entrance next to his home. It turned out he was the only one living on the island.

Besides having a small garden and a fish farm, this old fisherman had a pet frigate bird. The bird would spend many hours perched on a high fence overlooking our boat. It seemed he was very fascinated with me, for most likely he had never seen a cat before. His size intimidated me, so I never tried to get close to him. Still, I spent hours staring back at him, while he kept ruffling his feathers while squawking in a language that made no sense to me.

After a couple days, we moved on to another low atoll in the Tuamotus. Here we found a good passage inside to a well-protected anchorage. While I spent most of my time being lazy, Lee and Sheila went diving on some spectacular reefs that had all types of coral and colorful schools of fish. These fish didn't really go to school. That's just a term that means a large group of fish. Lee didn't catch any good eating fish, but Sheila and Elena

found a great collection of beautiful sea shells. I was happy to get a chance to play with some of the smaller cowrie shells that rolled easily when I batted them around.

The next day, just before sunset, we sailed off with pleasant trade winds for Tahiti in the Society Islands, which lay about 300 miles further west. The sunset was one of the nicest I have seen. I will never forget the brilliant changing colors as it dropped below the horizon while the full moon slowly rose up from the east. That vision was definitely one of the best visual celestial highlights of my time at sea. I purred a long time before falling to sleep.

CHAPTER 4
Life on Some
Trade Wind Islands

After a mostly uneventful but pleasant crossing lasting about three days, we arrived at the port of Papeete on the famous island of Tahiti. I was tired of just sleeping and chasing my tail, and glad to have some new surroundings with different forms of entertainment. It was here that we would clear in with officials, get some fresh provisions, explore the island, and make a change in crew. Elena was like an ocean hitchhiker who wanted to get on another boat, and our old friend Cindy was coming to join us from the States.

We were now in the largest seaport in this group of islands. There were plenty of cruising yachts tied stern to the shore with an anchor set out into deeper water off the bow. We found this method to be a common practice in this area. The crew only had to guide the dinghy a short distance along the rope to shore to get on land.

The French-governed Society Islands are a popular place for cruisers to visit and stock up with supplies. It was quite a change from the more remote and isolated islands we had recently visited. There were even cars driving down the roads. However, the highlight at this time of year was the preparation for a major holiday known as Bastille Day or La Fête. Besides all the musical performances and parties leading up to the holiday, there were lots of locals practicing racing their canoes in preparation for the inter-island competition. Although we would miss the actual holiday,

we did get to witness many of these practice races up close. One time while anchored at another island, a group of women paddled their canoe close by around our boat using us as the turning mark. Some laughed when they saw me watching them while I sauntered around on deck. I hoisted my front paws as if to wave.

Once Lee and Sheila had gotten some fresh produce from the local market and a few needed boat parts from a supply store, we moved on to a wonderful anchorage at Cooks Bay on the nearby island of Moorea. In the splendid anchorage surrounded by majestic volcanic mountains, we found a number of cruising yachts, a nice yacht club that provided musical entertainment, and a very large, modern, three-masted motor schooner anchored nearby. This boat was a very fancy tourist vessel owned by Club Med and had huge sails run by hydraulic motors. It was here that we changed crew members. Cindy was very excited to join us and immediately dove off the boat into the clear warm water for a swim. I sat on the bowsprit and enjoyed seeing how blissful and happy she was to be here.

After about a week of moving amongst a number of nice an-chorages within this group of islands, we came to the Bora Bora atoll. This is definitely one of the most spectacular island in all of the South Pacific and a place where no one is bored. There were plenty of parties for all the cruisers, and everyone had a grand time. I often got to be the center of attention when the sailors came to our boat. I think my ability to be a good companion and shipmate brought pleasure to each of them as I affectionately sat on their laps. When Sheila turned on the stereo music, I felt like dancing, but was getting too many pats to move.

After the crew had a fine time hiking up high in the hills for a great panoramic view of the anchorage below and diving in crystal-clear waters on nearby coral reefs, Lee announced it was time to move on to a new island nation, known as the Cook Islands. It was about 520 miles away to the west.

During this five-day crossing, the weather was mostly fine with light to moderate trade winds. Although our passage was pretty uneventful, Lee did catch a large mahi mahi. This was one

fish that we all loved to eat. The only humiliating thing was that Lee felt it necessary to hold me up right next to the fish for a photo. I was not happy about having my fur rub on the wet, slimy scales of the fish. It took me quite a while to lick the smell of fish off my fur, for I prefer to keep my fur clean and dry. However, I had no complaints when it came time for dinner.

The Cook Islands are divided into three distinct groups, each located many miles apart. We chose to head for Aitutaki, the island in the middle section that was closest to our intended route. It was home to a small population of Polynesians, who enjoyed a fair number of modern conveniences, because the island was a protectorate of New Zealand.

The entrance to the anchorage in the lagoon was on the west side of the island. The channel was marked with buoys, but the water depth was a bit shallow in certain places. While motoring halfway up the long channel, our boat hit the sandy bottom.

Although it did no damage, the sudden stop knocked Lee off balance, and he fell head over heels in the cockpit. I had to dash away, so he didn't land on me. Even though it was a close call, I had to laugh when I saw the look on his face. Luckily, he really never knew I was laughing, for it is hard for a cat to show that.

After waiting for the tide to rise and by running the motor full speed ahead, we eventually got free and made it to the deeper inner anchorage. We found out we could tie up with a line to a palm tree with the boat anchored only twenty feet from shore.

We soon learned that the young people on this island were famous for winning traditional dance competitions. Practice sessions were held in a nearby courtyard, and almost every evening, we had a front row seat for the entertainment. Music would fill the air as I fell asleep in the night. We often opened the boat to visitors, and Sheila served lots of cake and tea. Meanwhile, Cindy had fun spending time with some new island friends while I tried unsuccessfully to imitate some island dances. Even though I can be quite agile, my problem was that I kept stepping on my tail.

Besides visiting a site where a strange bearded lady ran unusual religious cult ceremonies and touring the island on rented scooters, Lee, Sheila, and Cindy enjoyed watching the local men play rugby. This sport can be very rough, and injuries are common. When visiting a graveyard near a local church, Sheila noticed a headstone that read "killed in a match accident."

Our time at the island was very pleasant. Sheila and Cindy played cards, entertained guest with sea stories, and talked with plenty of cruising friends on the marine radio. One day, Lee climbed the highest hill to get a good view of the beautiful blue lagoon, the surrounding outer reef, and the wide ocean beyond. He found it most fascinating to stand on his head and see how things looked from that point of view. Definitely not something a cat would ever think of doing. Humans like Lee sometimes do strange things.

When departing the island, Lee made sure it was high tide, so we could make it over the sand bar in the channel. Once we cleared the outer reef, we set sail for the islands of Samoa. It took us over five days to cover the distance of almost 800 miles on this crossing. We had now entered the latitudes further north and closer to the equator where the prevailing trade winds slightly shift the direction in which they blow due to a regional weather phenomena at this longitude. It is in this northern section of latitudes that cyclones generally develop, though it wasn't cyclone season. However, the weather was still variable with some rainstorms, shifting winds, and occasional wind squalls. Even so, we completed the crossing to Samoa without anything dramatic happening. After rounding some outer islands on the eastern side of the island group, we came to the port of Pago Pago, the capital of American Samoa on the main island of Tutuila.

CHAPTER 5

Fia Fia in Samoa

The Samoa Islands are divided into two groups—the more modernized American group to the east and the more traditional group of islands, known as Western Samoa, to the west. We decided to stop first in the American group, since it was along the way, and we could purchase some items we needed for the boat.

American Samoa is a U.S. territory and a great place to send and receive mail from the States. It also has a good supply of modern products and marine supplies. A fair number of cruising yachts gather here, and some of the American sailors can even find jobs. However, the harbor is not that interesting and is very dirty. The anchorage is adjacent to a number of tuna-fish factories, and the bottom of the anchorage had lots of sunken plastic garbage bags on it that make anchoring difficult, because the anchor can't dig in. Cruising yachts often drag anchor and end up drifting into other boats. The harbor had also been hit by some bad cyclones (basically the same as hurricanes), and we saw a number of derelict shipwrecked boats at rest along the shore.

The locals here seemed to have lost some of their traditional values and practices while also apparently eating too much American junk food, so there is an increasing problem with obesity. Even though I always prefer fresh fish over junk food, I still appreciated the availability of the good American dry cat food that is shipped to the port of Pago Pago. Since we had previously run out of such cat food, I was delighted to now have my bowl full. I even got some fresh milk to go with it. Although there was a limited supply of the fresh produce that Lee and Sheila prefer, the supermarkets were packed with other options that are unavailable in more remote places. They could now stock up on dry goods such as rice, pasta, beans, and flour. These items would keep for a long time.

Since there was little of real cultural interest, Lee and Sheila did not want to stay long in this place. After mate Cindy flew back home, they visited a nearby weather station and completed some work on the boat. Lee and Sheila were more interested in visiting places where the indigenous people lived in more traditional ways, so the next day, we departed for the islands in Western Samoa. After sailing only a short distance, we arrived in Apia, the capital seaport of Western Samoa on the island of Upolu.

Although many of the islanders in the South Pacific can speak English, it is always good to learn some of their own language. Sheila started learning especially the words for "hello" and "thank you." Meanwhile, I stayed with the universal cat "meow" language, while Lee often resorted to a silly form of sign language that made the locals laugh and wonder what he was trying to say. We soon found out that being friendly, respectful, and kind can go a long way in making friends, even when we didn't know the right words. Turns out that the locals here have a good word for the best way to live. The word is "fia fia," which means happy. That makes good sense to me!

When we cleared in with customs and immigration, one official asked to see our de-ratification certificate. Lee was surprised, as he had never had one, and he didn't know what to say. However, when the official saw me, he said no worries, for he considered me the "rat-control officer," so we did not need a paper certificate. Little did he know that I would most likely run from these large nasty rodents, especially if they were "pi-rats." And that is not the kind that eat pies.

Now in case you are wondering, cats (especially female felines) have long been employed on trading ships to protect their precious cargo from invasive pests or vermin like the rodents that will eat just about everything while leaving disgusting droppings and smelly urine. Rats were considered a major problem, and over the centuries, certain cats were considered very useful shipmates and mascots that also brought good luck and comfort for the crew. Some of these cats could kill and eat many rats, thereby saving the ship's food supply from being damaged. The rats also provided food that was full of protein for those hungry cats.

Although I had developed a taste for mice in my youth, I soon became spoiled by my preference for fish while at sea. Some of the rats I did see were also too big and intimidating, and my nose and whiskers would often curl up in distaste. Since our ship was small and we never had a real issue with rats on the boat, I was happily relieved of any responsibility in completing any rat-control duties.

After we passed the inspection, Lee and Sheila ventured ashore to check out the town and get some fresh produce at a large outdoor marketplace. Unlike American Samoa, the fresh fruit and veggies were not imported, overripe, and rotting. The island's volcanic soil was a great natural resource that enabled productive farmlands. There was plenty of fresh, tasty produce to choose from, and Lee and Sheila loaded up on bananas, papayas, limes, breadfruit, pineapples, mangos, melons, and an assortment of green veggies. Later they met with other cruisers, took rides on funky, old, brightly colored buses, watched a local marching band perform, and made more new friends.

One of the highlights of our stay was the many canoe races that took place. One day we were very surprised to see what had to be the world's longest canoe. It had about thirty men paddling, while a fellow in the stern beat a rhythm on a big drum. It went very fast as they raced about the harbor. I waved hello to them with my forepaw, but only one of the preoccupied crew saw me and smiled.

Lee and Sheila also spent a good part of the time with other sailors and went on land trips to other villages around the island. They were greeted warmly by the local people. Some would even invite them into their homes for tea. The locals seemed to be very curious about visitors from away, especially when they were living in a more remote location.

During one hike into the jungle, Lee and Sheila found a nice waterfall that emptied into a pond by the sea. They went for a refreshing swim and had a delightful time soaking in the cool cascade of fresh water. When they later told me this while I sat on the hot deck, I had to admit it sounded quite refreshing.

CHAPTER 6
In an Island Village

We decided to move on to explore some other anchorages around the island. After a few days of anchoring at some pleasant locations, Lee noticed on the chart that there was a perfectly protected cove with a village on the southwest side of the island. This looked like a good place for a final stop before heading further south to the islands in Tonga, and the village of Sataoa would become our home away from home in Western Samoa. After we arrived and anchored near the small village, we went below to eat and rest. Soon, we heard a knock on the hull. We found that two young boys had arrived in a canoe, and one handed us a note from the pastor of the local church. He had heard that a storm was coming and wanted to invite us to come ashore for safety at his home. This was very nice of him, but since we would rather be with the boat in case of bad weather, we gratefully declined the offer. This was the first sign that we would have a wonderful time here with very warm-hearted people.

The storm was not that bad, and after it passed by the next day, the friendly boys returned to our boat. We invited them aboard for tea and cookies. Although they had never seen a cruising yacht like ours, they were more interested in me and desperately wanted to hold and pat me. I am happy to say they were purrfect at it.

During our wonderful stay of over a week, we had many visitors on the boat, and Lee and Sheila spent plenty of time in the village, often sharing what we had and trading for many gifts.

The tradition of gift giving is a strong part of the local culture. The act of giving seems to have a circular effect, for as one person gives something to another, they will in return give something to someone else. This practice also has the added benefit of reducing the need to have cash for buying things.

Lee spent time watching some men build a dugout canoe with just hand tools. He was amazed that it took only three days to complete the process. Lee also played games with the kids, while Sheila learned about local cooking, helped women do their laundry in the river, and got to sit down with the ladies and weave her own mat. Most of the women spent many hours making woven mats that were used as beds, for wall hangings, and as gifts for honored guests. Meanwhile, I got lots of pats, even good ones from the children. The chief was very kind and invited us to church on Sunday. Since very few travelers or cruisers come here, all the locals seemed happy to have us around. A few young men became fast friends, and the chief even offered to have a small house built for us if we would stay. Since Lee and Sheila had no children, one couple offered to let us adopt a baby. Well, that was most unusual to our western way of thinking, but it's a way of binding people together in kinship in the Polynesian culture. However, I did not like the idea, as I had no desire to live with a crying baby.

One day, Lee and Sheila decided to walk to the next town to get something at a store. It took them longer than expected, and by midday they were still walking while it was very hot. The people living along the road had more sense and were resting in the shade. When they saw the foreigners walking, they would gesture them to come in out of the sun and have something cold to drink. Lee and Sheila felt like fools for walking at this time of day. Later someone reminded them of the old saying "only mad dogs and Englishmen go out in the midday sun." Anyone with

good common sense, including a cat like me, would know better. I guess mad dogs lack common sense. I am not sure why Englishmen are mad.

As the days passed by, we continued to enjoy ourselves living a good life. Since coconuts are an important food source for these people, we were very curious about how it was prepared. One young man showed us how they were collected by climbing up a coconut tree in his bare feet. His feet looked wide with big toes, likely because he had been doing this for years. However, the trick to climbing straight up so high required the addition of a piece of twine that was twisted around both his feet to hold them together and keep them from slipping. Even though he was able to go up the tree very quickly, I was not that impressed. With my strong claws, I bet I could have done it faster. But though I do like to be up high, I would have had difficulty getting back down.

When he got to the top, he collected the coconuts, put them in a bag, and lowered them with a rope to the ground, then slid down effortlessly. After his descent, the coconuts were put in a

pile next to a seat where another man had a machete and a sharp stick driven into the ground. With the nut secured to the sharp stick, he used the machete to cut the coconut husk apart and expose the inner nut. After cracking the nut open and pouring the coconut milk into a bowl for drinking, he proceeded to shave off the white inner coconut meat with a sharp metal hand tool. Once he had collected enough of the coconut meat, it was squeezed through the fibers from the outside of the coconut shell, making a soft cream that filled another bowl. This coconut cream was used in many different traditional dishes that would often include either fish or pig. I am happy to say that I did get to taste some fish with coconut cream. It was yummy for the tummy.

Many great feasts were served during our stay, and our hearts grew fond of these gracious island people. The only thing that I ever complained about was the lack of good kitty litter for my cat box. Since we had been unable to find any for a while, Sheila had to use sand or newspaper. I did not like either choice. The newspaper was too slippery and often became wet to the touch, and the sand would stick in my paws. Since neither reduced the smell of what I left behind, I would often dash above on deck for fresh air and shake my paws, much to the dismay of Lee and Sheila.

Well, the life of a sea cat has its ups and downs. To be honest, I feel I must mention both the good and bad parts. But since I have learned to adapt to most of these conditions, I cannot complain too much.

When our time in Samoa came to an end, we found it difficult to leave our new friends. There were lots of hugs and gift giving. Lee and Sheila were given a fine mat, some local artifacts, and custom clothes to wear. I got a nice native necklace, but since it drove me nuts swinging about too much, I had to remove it. Anyway, it's the thought that counts.

After the boat was loaded with fresh veggies and fruit, we were ready to go. One of the locals, who had become a dear friend, was so sad we were leaving that he could not watch us depart. He knew it was unlikely that he'd see us again.

Both Lee and Sheila would never like to say goodbye, but instead said "See you later." They would leave the idea of returning uncertain, for they never really knew for sure. Such is our life when traveling from one paradise island to another.

CHAPTER 7
New Potatoes

After a day and half sailing south, we came to our first island stop in the Kingdom of Tonga. Yes, this really is a monarchy with an actual king and queen. It was the only one we ever visited while cruising around the world. Tonga consists of a long chain of islands that extends many miles to the south from the northern-most island of Niuatoputapu, which visitors sometimes call "New Potatoes" as that is easier to say. This turned out to be another place where we would stay a while.

Many of the islands in Tonga began as volcanoes. However, most, including this one, are now dormant. The peaceful Tongans lead simple lives close to nature—fishing and farming—and are very friendly with the fair number of cruisers that visit New Potatoes. We were immediately taken in by a local man who learned English by talking to cruisers. He prepared a grand feast for all visiting sailors, provided entertainment with local girls performing traditional dances, and told us many stories about Tonga and their king. Lee was able to go diving with local fisherman, while some women gave Sheila more lessons on making traditional mats out of strips of pandanus leaves. The making of these mats is a time-consuming process, and the women in the village make plenty of them throughout the year. The finest mats are used as gifts or for ceremonial clothing worn by the elders. There was often a competition to see who made the best ones.

As with many Polynesian islands, sharing and trading is a constant pastime. Everyone on the island is like part of one big extended family, and children refer to many of the adults as "papa" or "mama," not just their parents. A cruising couple we met had actually adopted two young Tongan girls without any problem.

It was here that Lee and Sheila got their first taste of a mild narcotic called kava. Kava is a drink prepared from the root of a local plant and consumed in ceremonies and special gatherings. It is used in a number of island groups throughout the western Pacific, and every country has certain rules about how it is used. Although it is not an alcohol, kava has a certain intoxicating effect on those who drink it. Most often participants become very silly, happy, and lazy. Ceremonies with kava drinking often last long into the night. Once I did try a sip of it, but since it tasted like dirty dishwater, I quickly spit it out. I am already a lazy cat who can be happy without it.

Another custom event that is very entertaining is the traditional dancing that happens periodically. The dances include both male and female participants dressed up in special costumes. The audience is encouraged to give money to the dancers that they most appreciate. The dancers' bare arms and legs are coated with oil so that the money can be stuck on their bodies. Musicians support the dancers with sweet, melodic songs. I have to admit that the sounds of this music did make me dance around on deck. I was able to keep my tail flying high.

Since we were all having so much fun and I was getting lots of good pats and loving attention from visiting cruisers, we ended up staying at New Potatoes for almost a month. During this time, Lee and Sheila explored various parts of the island. One day, they joined a group of sailors for a hike up the nearby mountain. When they finally got to the top, all of them were very hot and tired. They also found themselves being attacked by many mosquitos. The local guide took pity on them and cut up some coconuts for a refreshing drink. After resting and admiring the view of a nearby volcanic island, they went back down to the village. It definitely seems that all excursions into the interior of islands have their ups and downs.

Although there weren't many wild critters, there were plenty of domestic animals around. Most everyone raised their own pigs, an important part of the Tongan diet. Pigs are also handy for clearing brush from the yard since they love to chew things. Chickens were abundant and of course their meat and eggs are a useful source of food. There were also a number of scrawny dogs that didn't seem to serve any particular purpose other than barking. I was glad they couldn't come aboard and bother me.

The only other animals that we often saw were goats. These curious animals seemed a bit goofy to me. However, my impression of them changed when I got to see them during a fight close to shore. These goats had long horns on their heads and would make a loud cracking noise when they jumped up and rammed each other with their heads.

When it comes to sea life, there wasn't much that I encountered while lazing around on the boat at anchor. But sitting on deck staring into the water, I often wondered which fish swimming by would taste the best. Meanwhile, Lee had some good times going diving with some of the locals in their small fishing boats. On one occasion, the fishermen were intent on finding some octopus. This was usually accomplished by allowing the octopus to attach its tentacles to a diver's arm, whereupon they would swim back to the surface with their catch.

Though many of the natives consider octopus a delicacy, some did not care for it. As for me, I had no interest in eating these ugly, slimy looking creatures, especially since they taste like rubber. Lee also agreed with me and stayed clear of the divers when they were trying to catch them. When under attack, an octopus

would often spray a black, ink-like fluid as some sort of defense. More reason to stay away.

One interesting thing about the inhabitants of Niuatoputapu is that they are not afraid of sharks. The locals often swim with sharks, and some would even hunt them for food. Turns out there is a local myth or belief that there is a sea god that protects them from sharks. Therefore, no one is scared of them, and there have been no reports of shark attacks. Now this seems amazing to me. However, Lee thought he knew the real reason why this is so. He said sharks are very good at sensing fear, and if no fear is recognized in their prey, then they would lose interest and go away. Well, that may be true, but I was not about to test his theory. I am really a scaredy cat and would always stay away from anything so big and mean looking. Anyway, as long as I stayed out of the water, I had nothing to worry about.

CHAPTER 8
Difficult Moments

Before our stay in New Potatoes came to an end, two things happened that changed my level of contentment. The first thing actually affected Lee instead of me.

One day, he had planned to go fishing with the men, but when he came to the house where they were to meet, he found only the women were present. The men had already left without him. To make up for his disappointment, the women invited him for lunch. Well, that was sweet of them. Since he didn't want to be ungrateful, he stayed and waited for lunch to cook. When the meal was served, Lee was surprised to see two ugly lumps

of something he did not recognize. It turned out to be some sea slugs, also known as sea cucumbers. When he started to eat, he found that they tasted like a burnt rubber tire, and he had to chew for a long, long time. It was the worst lunch he had ever had. Before long, he was considering how to get out of this situation. He told the women that he had had a big breakfast and was really was not that hungry. From the look on his face, I don't think he fooled them. He left as soon as he could, while making a point of thanking them.

On another occasion Sheila invited a group of young boys out for cookies and tea. They had been wanting to see the boat and the big fat cat that lived there. Sheila should have known better, for I was not happy about this. I think she thought that I needed some excitement and that I had not been getting much exercise while laying around. Well, I disagree! When the boys advanced on my comfortable position, I had to run. It seemed like hours went by while they chased me all around the boat. Some eventually did catch me, but soon afterwards I was able to break free and hide where they could not find me. Realizing my anguish and

humiliation, Sheila decided to keep them occupied with eating cookies. Even though she later gave me some evaporated milk to cheer me up, I would have preferred some catnip to lift my spirits.

A short time later, we had a nice party with the other cruisers and said goodbye to the friendly folks on the island. It was time to head further south to the main port of Vava'u on the larger island of Neiafu. It took almost two days to complete this 300-mile crossing. The weather was mixed, with periods of rain and winds that were either too strong or light. On one day when conditions were fair, it was Lee's turn again for a frustrating experience.

Around midafternoon, a sea bird landed on the top of the mizzen mast, which is the smaller mast at the stern of the boat. After a while, Lee noticed that the bird kept dropping bird turds on the deck from his perch aloft. Lee knew that these turds are hard to clean up and soon decided that the bird had had enough rest and should leave the boat. He went aft and shook the rigging wire hoping that would make the bird fly away. Since it had little effect, he started yelling at the bird. Still, no effect. He then dug out some water balloons and threw them at the bird. The bird just calmly looked at Lee without moving an inch. In the end, Lee found a long narrow piece of tubing, climbed the rigging up near the top of the mast, and waved it at the bird. The bird now realized his time of rest was over and flew away, but not without depositing a few more turds as a final gift. I think the bird must have eaten too many fish that day.

The next day, when we arrived in the busy harbor of Vava'u, we found a large anchorage with a crowd of cruising yachts that came from all over the world. After meeting with the local officials and going to the market for fresh produce, Lee and Sheila proceeded to have a reunion with other cruisers that they knew. It is amazing how many friends you can make when sailing around the world. Sometimes you sail along for months at a time with other cruisers who are taking the same route. Sometimes they go a different way, and you don't see them again until a year later at some distant location. This keeps it interesting for cruising cats and sailors who travel for long periods of time on the high seas.

While in Vava'u, we heard more stories about the king and queen of Tonga. Turns out the king is a very large man, who one time had a chance to visit the U.S. During his visit, he was introduced to American fast food. When he went to McDonald's, he tried some hamburgers and found that he liked them a lot. The story goes that he was able to eat about twenty of them before he was full. I guess he was so big that it took that many to fill him up. But who knows if that story is true or not.

As a cat, I never developed a taste for burgers. I have always been a fish lover, and was most jealous when one day Lee and Sheila returned to the boat raving about the great tuna steaks they had had at a local restaurant. They could have at least brought me a taste. It would have been much better than the bothersome invading moth I had eaten earlier.

My frustration with the recent lack of fresh fish did not go away. But my discontent with lack of a proper diet was soon replaced by distress and embarrassment. It seems that Lee and

Sheila were getting concerned about my safety and felt that I needed some survival training in how to get back on the boat in case I should again fall overboard into the water. Now that is all well and good, but there should have been a better way to accomplish the instruction.

To my surprise, the first step was to throw me overboard. Lee had hung a net over the rail and hoped that I would see it and use the net to climb back on the boat. But when I first surfaced and saw the dinghy floating next to the stern of the boat, I swam in earnest to it and clawed my way up on top. From there, I was able to easily jump back on deck.

Lee was not satisfied with my choice and deposited me back in the water. This time, he guided me with a boat hook, forcing me to swim toward the net. I had no choice but to try and climb it. After some difficulty, I succeeded and was then rewarded with a dry towel and some hugs. Even though the water was warm and we were in a protected harbor, I was definitely not happy and let everyone know about it. I hoped that since I had passed the test, it would not happen again. It took me a long time to lick my paws and fur dry.

It turned out that all my screaming and splashing around had caught the attention of other sailors anchored in the harbor. Some of them had taken a closer look at us through their binoculars and were very concerned. Glad to say that later on some of them complained to Lee about his actions. Little did they know it was really my safety he was concerned with. Still, I was not pleased with his methods and was glad that no sharks were nearby.

Lee later informed me that back in the past, sailors on tall ships often employed numerous, ingenious, and sometime desperate ways to rescue cats that fell overboard or were swept off by a wave into the sea. Besides using nets, oars, or baskets, some sailors even dove into the water to grab the shivering, terrified cat and bring her back aboard the boat. It was said that one sailor did this by carrying the cat in his mouth with his teeth, holding the waterlogged cat around the scruff (back side) of the neck so his hands were free to swim back to the ship. In any case, if conditions were rough, it was especially difficult to actually locate the cat floating in the huge rolling seas as she drifted away while frantically trying to swim back.

Although this rescue story was impressive, it did little to comfort me. After all, even though I am very agile and have a good sense of balance, I knew by experience that I had to be careful not to slip when on deck. Even if I could be rescued, I didn't want to experience another exhausting, soaking-wet occurrence like this. I promised to stay below when sailing in a storm if there were no more training exercises. I usually do that anyway!

CHAPTER 9
Remarkable Times in Tonga

I am happy to say that most of my time in Tonga was really enjoyable. I got to spend it by either being the center of attention or simply watching others carry on doing silly things. We spent a few months slowly cruising through these islands while stopping at remote anchorages, often where only small villages were located.

Lee and Sheila usually invited people aboard the boat for snacks, storytelling, or some music on the tape player. It was common for everyone to exchange gifts. However, I think the best gift was a good sense of humor. Laughing and teasing seemed to be a popular pastime here. There was no shortage of silliness, especially when Lee would join his goofy antics with those of the locals. Except when his unusual foreign appearance made some babies cry, Lee made most of the children (and me) laugh at his theatrics.

On certain occasions, I found the locals more amusing than Lee. Once when a group of women were on the boat, one lady grabbed a freshly caught, uncooked fish and put it in her mouth so Lee could take her picture. I must admit she looked very silly. But I would have likely done the same thing if the fish had been cooked and its scales removed.

Still, that was nothing compared to Halloween in Tonga. That is mostly an American holiday, and the local Tongans knew nothing about it. Lee had kept a few masks on the boat and brought them out to enhance the celebration. He invited some native Tongans to come with him to a cruisers' party at a local yacht club onshore. The cruisers dressed up in costumes, and Lee shared

his masks with the locals. Everyone had a great time. I later heard that one of the cruisers even wore a cat outfit. Probably didn't look as good as me. As a real cat, I had no need for a mask, and nobody tried to put one on me. I would have been quite annoyed if they did.

There were a number of activities that were new to the cruisers, and many of them were invited to join in the celebrations and be a part of these traditional events. Tongans often had communal feasts for special occasions, and if guests (like us) were present, they were encouraged to eat first. The primary foods served were pig, fish, chicken, rice, and taro, along with other fruits and vegies. Pigs and fish were usually cooked in an "umu," which is an earth oven in which the food is buried on top of hot rocks and covered with banana leaves to steam. This preferred method of baking makes for wonderfully tasty results and is often used throughout the South Pacific, since modern cooking stoves are rare possessions in this part of the world. Coconut cream is often

added to many seafood dishes, and when added to cooked papaya fruit, it makes a very delicious desert.

Another activity that was popular with Tongans was going to church. Most of the folks were devout Christians, but the way they worshipped was different than what we had seen before. All would first dress up in traditional outfits with woven mats tied around the waist as a sign of respect. The men often started with a small ceremony where they drank kava. Since this practice was often included on other ceremonial occasions, it seemed only natural that they would combine it with Sunday worship. When people got to church, there would be plenty of singing and dancing, and some women would wave fans to help participants stay cool when it was hot. It made for a very lively and enjoyable service and a lot more fun than some other boring forms of worship that I had previously heard about. Lee and Sheila were often invited to church services, and when they dressed up with similar traditional attire, the locals showed great appreciation. Showing respect for local traditions always brings honor to all participants. Even though I never dressed up to look like the locals, I am glad to say that I was still appreciated. My natural calico outfit of orange with some brown and white spots of fur was colorful enough.

As the weeks passed by, Lee said that it was nearing the time to depart for our next destination, New Zealand. Soon it would be the season when hurricanes would be developing in the area, and we wanted no part of that. New Zealand was far enough south to be free of these weather disturbances.

However, we still had a few more stops to make before setting out on that long-distance crossing. Lee wanted to stop at one island that was known to have some good caves and a variety of bats. When looking around on shore, he had no trouble finding those bats. Besides living in dark caves, hundreds of them were also hanging upside down in the branches of trees. We found out that the bats in the caves were called vampire bats. I was glad not to get close to them. The bats in the trees were called fruit bats. I guess they only liked to eat fruit instead of drinking blood.

During the explorations on land, Lee and Sheila got to see a number of owls and hawks. But what really got their attention were the wild boars, which I guess are a meaner distant relative of pigs and often roam around freely in the bush. Both Lee and Sheila kept their distance from these crazy, wild-looking creatures, for they can run very fast.

On one of the last short daysails between the islands, we passed a few small islands where volcanoes were still somewhat active. However, there were no major eruptions at that time. The only thing we saw rising high was a large splash of water that burst upward from a spouting rock as we sailed close by the shore.

We even saw the island where Captain Bligh landed in his small boat after sailing for weeks, covering many miles from the point where he was cast off from his ship the *Bounty* by its mutinous crew. During our voyage around the world, we often came across historical sites from the distant past that recalled famous ocean explorers like Captain Cook. It seems we were now following in some of their footsteps on our long voyage.

Before long, we arrived at Nuku'alofa on the island of Tongatapu, which was to be our last stop in Tonga. This fair-sized town is the capital of Tonga. Lee and Sheila quickly made some friends while getting the boat ready for the next long crossing. After they purchased some provisions at the store, the son of a friendly New Zealand couple that Sheila had previously contacted through the ham radio took them on a tour of the island. His name was Simon, and he expressed interest in joining us for the next ocean crossing to his home in New Zealand for Christmas. After some deliberation and radio contact with his parents, who were already home on leave from work in Tonga, Lee agreed to take him on. Simon was both a good sailor and an excellent diver. However, he was a bit slow in taking care of business, and it was at the last moment, after we had already cleared customs, that he finally got his own clearance, and jumped aboard. We set sail the next day.

Although there is no real island along the long route to New Zealand, there is one small, isolated anchorage in a tiny atoll lagoon called Minerva Reef. It is a good anchorage with lots of excellent places for diving on the surrounding outer reef. However, it is only accessible when the weather is fair, for the reef is very low and rough seas could wash right over it, especially during high tide. Someone had given us a chart so we could find the entrance, but we would need to take care when entering. I was glad that we had some other yachts sailing along the same route to this location. It definitely made me feel more secure having them close by. Even though I wasn't really concerned and trusted my captain, I didn't want to end up shipwrecked in the middle of nowhere. Sometimes my imagination gets the better of me.

The crossing to Minerva Reef covered a distance of about 280 miles, which meant it would likely take us just a couple days to get there. The weather was fine on the day we left, and I am happy to say it stayed that way during the whole trip. Simon was a good mate, and everyone was excited to be moving on.

It is important to realize that sailors can sometimes get restless and in need of excitement when simply sailing along without any other activities to entertain them. It is not that they are bored, but more like they just want to play. Lee and Sheila now had a good collection of Polynesian music on tapes that they had recorded on different islands during the previous months in the tropics. They often played these songs while sailing along or when visitors came aboard.

I am not really sure who got the idea first, but before I realized what was happening, Lee and Simon decided they would use me for some extra entertainment. They came up with the idea of somehow making me dance to the music. Now this did not sound right to me. But since they gave me no warning and as a cat I could not say no, they proceeded to organize things.

They decided to dress me up in a traditional Polynesian outfit with a grass skirt, small coconut bra, a shell necklace, and a straw hat. Now this was absurd, but what could I do but play along. Lee turned on some different island tunes, and Simon lifted me up from behind and made me move my paws and hips in the correct way to the music. Meanwhile, Lee filmed the dance with his video camera.

Now even though it first seemed comical even to me, I got very tired and irritated as it went on song after song. They kept going for what seemed like far too long. I was now getting weary and mad. When I hissed, they just laughed, for they said I looked so cute. Oh great, just what I needed!

I guess it was Sheila who first became sympathetic and asked them to stop. Soon after that, they said okay and untangled me from my outfit. Once I was set free, I stumbled to get my footing and then quickly scampered away and jumped below to hide. Never again! If I were ever that bored or restless, I would be satisfied with just chasing my tail or playing with loose rope.

PART 2

Down Under and
Back to the Tropics

CHAPTER 10
A Cold Ocean Crossing

I am glad the rest of our crossing had no more humiliating moments for me. I was even rewarded with another bird, called a sea tern, landing on the boat's railing. Now this was more like it! I really needed someone else (not human) to play with. But although I did attempt to get close to the bird and take a few swipes at him, I soon gave that up, knowing that if I continued, I might be closer to falling overboard. I resigned myself to simply watching and sharpening my claws on some wood while the bird ruffled his feathers and shook his head.

The next morning, we arrived at Minerva Reef, and conditions were perfect for finding the entrance. Once inside, Lee watched out for coral heads while Sheila motored the boat to a good location for anchoring amongst a group of other cruising yachts. Lee decided we should stay a while and go diving for fish with other sailors on the following day.

The next day, the weather was still fine, so a group of sailors gathered all their fishing gear, got into their dinghies, and headed out to one of the nearby deep-water reefs outside the inner lagoon.

The reef they chose to dive on was like a mound that rose up from the deep. The top of it was shallow enough that each dinghy could anchor above it and stay in position, while each diver went down with spear in hand to search for fish. Lee decided he would first stay near the dinghy as Simon took his turn to swim down and spear some fish. Lee watched Simon through his diving mask while treading water on the surface by the dinghy.

It was not long before Lee became concerned when he noticed some intruders, for a group of sharks had appeared on the scene. They moved in around Simon and proceeded to circle him. Simon had previously told Lee that he was not afraid of sharks and simply rotated around with his spear pointed at the circling sharks. Well, Lee was not that confident in this situation and did not dare dive down to help him. I guess the sharks were intimidated by Simon's spear, for eventually they left. Thank goodness!! It was not long afterwards that a number of the divers, including Simon, had caught plenty of nice fish for dinner. This included some tuna, mackerel, kingfish, snapper, and grouper. After dinner that night, I was a happy cat with a full belly and purred for a long time while stretching out very contented on my bunk.

The next morning, we and another boat decided it was time to leave for New Zealand, which was about 900 miles away to

the south. We would now be going further "down under." That means we were going down under the equator into the temperate weather zone below the area where the trade winds blow. This was going to be the furthest south in latitude we would ever go in the southern hemisphere. We would now have different weather conditions, with the possibility of cold fronts moving across our path. It was likely that we could have winds blowing from the east as well as from the west. Captain Lee had to calculate the odds and decide on the best heading to sail in the shortest period of time. After considering whether to set the course more to the east or west, he decided to take a direct path. As it turned out this was a good decision.

For the first few days, all went well. But eventually we got our first cold front, and since all of us were not used to such weather after months in the tropics, it was time to bundle up. Sheila, who was very sensitive to the cold, kept putting on more clothes as the air temperature dropped. She soon had so much clothing on that

you could hardly recognize her. I was happy that I had a thick coating of fur and was content to lie on her lap while she was at the helm.

Over the remaining days, we had variable conditions with winds sometimes in our favor. Other times we had to sail close to the wind with waves splashing over the boat. Still, our path took us close to our desired route. The days passed quickly, while the crew took turns sleeping, standing watch, and eating. The one part of day we always shared together was around sunset at dinner time.

I must say that Sheila's ability to cook dinner on the boat is beyond amazing. When you consider how much the boat moves about while sailing over the waves, you might wonder how it was possible. What really helped this process was the design of the stove, because it was mounted on gimbals that allowed it to swing on its mounts and thereby stay on the level. Although we did not have to worry about pots and pans flying off the stove top while sailing in the rolling seas, the cook still had to be very adept at handling all the ingredients while the boat heeled over and bounced along. With my own paws, I applaud Sheila's ability to complete this task and provide me with a happy, full belly.

When we were getting close to land, maybe a day away from the northern end of New Zealand, we had a wonderful surprise. Two large whales came by and jumped high out of the water. I think they were welcoming us to the area. After spouting water high above and dancing about for a while, they departed south. Maybe they were showing us the way. Fine by me!

Around midday, we had another surprise come out of the blue. A large albatross appeared over the horizon and headed for the boat. When it came close, this magnificent bird flew a few times around our mast but did not land. These sea birds are quite famous and native to the Southern Ocean. It has been said that they bring good luck. I was glad to hear that.

The next day, we spotted land early in the morning. It was Aotearoa, the land of the long white cloud, which is the name of New Zealand in the native Maori language. The high mountains were still a fair distance away, but Lee calculated that we would be at a sheltered anchorage before darkness fell that evening. I was happy about that, for I longed to be in calm waters again. We had been at sea for over seven days, and that evening we made it to an anchorage and slept peacefully in calm waters. Even though this was a welcome change, I found myself having difficulty walking normally after spending so much time swaying to and fro and wobbling about on the rolling ocean waves.

CHAPTER 11
The New Zealand Cat Patrol

We were now in Kiwi Land, a country far from the rest of the world. The word "kiwi" is a nickname used for the inhabitants that comes from the delicious kiwi fruit that grows there. There is also a kiwi bird that is native to this area and considered to be as smart as the local parrot called a kea.

New Zealand is what is called a first-world country with all the modern conveniences, in contrast to the third-world remote islands we previously visited, where the people have fewer possessions. All the crew were now looking forward to hot showers, laundromats, and other amenities that they had previously done without. This large island nation also has much to offer visitors—friendly people, healthful living standards, cultural attractions, and splendid scenery. In addition, it is home to the indigenous Maori people, who have lived here for ages and still perform lively traditional dances and ceremonies. They are also known for having an extensive number of artistic tattoos all over their bodies. Lee and Sheila were excited to be here and were looking forward to exploring the two principal large islands in this country. As for Simon, he could have cared less about that and was anxious to leave for home. That was fine by me, for I would love to replace him with a kiwi bird.

Upon our arrival in the port city of Whangarei, we found a good yacht marina where we could moor the boat and were warmly greeted by many other cruisers. However, we soon had to deal with a new problem. It turns out that this country has strict rules about visiting animals. Since there is no rabies here, the officials do not want any animals bringing it into their country. Even if there is a cat like me that does not have any rabies, there are no exceptions to this rule.

This basically means that no animals are allowed to come ashore and must be kept under local observation in quarantine on their boat. Well, even though I had no intention of going ashore, the officials from MAF (Ministry of Agriculture and Fisheries) still felt it necessary to make sure I did not leave the boat. A periodic boat inspection was considered necessary to ensure that all cats were always on our boats. We were even given a special green flag to identify us as a "cat boat." As it turned out, there were eight other boats with cats. We all wondered how this would work out. In the end, arrangements were made to have all the cat boats moored close to each other for the convenience of the patrolling inspector, who would periodically row by in his dinghy to see if all cats were present and accounted for. I was amazed to see so many sea cats from all around the world so close by. I have to say none looked as cute as me.

Anyway, I really had no problem with this confinement, since I am content to stay on the boat. I also appreciated getting the attention, for I always like to be recognized as a great sea cat. The situation was more of a problem for Lee and Sheila, since they wanted to do some traveling on land away from the boat. However, they were soon able to make arrangements with other cruising friends to care for me while they were gone.

Before that time came, there was plenty for them to do while remaining on the boat. After cleaning the salt off the boat with a freshwater hose and putting things in order, they went for hot showers followed by some shopping at a local supermarket. Sheila came back with plenty of good food for everyone, including me.

She raved about the amazing choices that were available. After drooling over all the tasty options, Lee got a nice coffee ice cream shake and finished it off later with blueberries and whipped cream. I got some of my favorite fresh milk for the first time in months. I also stole a few good licks of whipped cream when Lee wasn't looking.

Since we had to pay the cat inspector for the time it took him to do his job, the next time he returned to check on me, Sheila decided on a way to make things go faster. When the inspector rowed closer to our boat, she hoisted me up high so he could quickly see me before rowing off to the next boat. For some reason, she felt it more entertaining to take my front paw and make me wave to the inspector. Okay, if you must!

Inspections soon became a normal thing, and most of the sailors on cat boats adapted their daily schedule to this. I think the inspector actually only came by once every three days, so that made things easier. Many of the sailors would find a caretaker for their cat and take trips around the island for a period of days or

weeks. One time, a couple on a boat had to make special arrangements since they had no one to look after their cat and had to lock the boat. They told the inspector that their cat always stayed in the same spot on a bunk down below. They told him that all he had to do was look in the porthole and see the cat sitting there as proof he was on the boat. So the next time he came, the inspector looked below and saw the cat. All was fine. The next time he came, the cat was still there. However, later on during one inspection, the officer became puzzled. He now realized that the cat always sat the same way and never moved.

Well as it turned out, it was a practical joke. The cat was not a real cat, but a stuffed fake cat. The inspector was mortified when the word got out to the local newspaper and it became the joke around town. In the end, the inspector had to laugh at himself.

CHAPTER 12
Following Our Dreams in Kiwi Land

Since we had about five southern summer months for our stay in New Zealand, there was plenty of time to play around and explore. We now had lots of fellow cruisers for neighbors at the marina, and we had not seen some of our sailor friends for months. It was time for some great reunions, and Lee and Sheila hosted many gatherings on our boat for both locals and cruisers. Again, I got to be the center of attention with lots of good pats. It was another "purrfect" time for me to follow my dreams and relax a lot.

Besides having plenty of new choices of good cat food from the supermarket, I had ample time to sleep without worrying about being rolled around by the waves. When sleeping, I also found that my dreams changed in a strange way. I soon found out that New Zealand has more sheep than people and that sheep-herding is a common occupation. I am not sure why this made such an impact on me, but I soon found myself often dreaming of sheep. Maybe it was simply because I liked these friendly, furry animals.

Lee and Sheila also followed their dreams and soon took off on a tour of New Zealand. They got a special tourist package ticket for trips by bus, boat, and train around both islands. They had a great time seeing the sights and staying at youth hostels and guest bungalows. Besides finding numerous sheep in the fields, they saw plenty of beautiful flowering plants, wildlife, rivers, and snow-capped mountains, including Aoraki, also known as Mount Cook, named after the famous explorer. They also swam in hot springs, took a kayak trip up a river, and visited historical museums

in different towns. They got to meet some Maori people, who lived on the land long before the British explorers came during the last century. These indigenous people were very friendly and talented. While adapting over the years to living with changes in the modern world, their traditional ways have still been well preserved.

Lee and Sheila also found some unique activities that were available for tourists. This included bungee jumping and paragliding. These activities are definitely for brave people. Bungee jumping is done from a bridge or cliff high above the ground. The tourists first attach a flexible line to their feet. Then, with some coaxing, each person is required to jump head first, descending all the way down until close to the ground below, where the flexible, rubbery line stops them and bounces them back up. Well, Lee, who is afraid of heights, decided that this was not his cup of tea and simply watched others accomplish this feat. That makes sense to me, for I would never want to try it. I would likely meow in distress all the way down.

Paragliding is another type of activity that starts up high. In this case the starting point is most often a mountain top or high hill. Individuals are strapped into a type of glider that has wings. A local supervising instructor is also attached to the glider in a position where he or she can direct its path through the air and keep an eye on the passenger secured in a harness. Both individuals start by running off the edge of the mountain top into the open space. The glider catches the wind and flies off over a long distance to the valley far below. Lee thought about this thrilling activity, but again declined to take part. Watching others do it was fun enough for him.

Meanwhile, the only jumping and flying that I did was in my dreams. I was also well cared for by a cruiser friend from a nearby yacht while Lee and Sheila were away. When they did return, I heard all the stories of their adventures. Soon after that, it was time for celebrating Christmas and the New Year, and there were lots of good barbecues and parties.

Early in January, Lee did get to fly. However, this time it was on a regular airplane back home to the States to take care of some business. He took lots of boxes of souvenirs back with him.

After returning, Lee declared it was now time to haul the boat out at the local boat yard and get the bottom of the hull painted with the special antifouling paint that would keep barnacles from growing there.

Well, this seemed okay with me until I learned that I had to be locked up down below in the boat while this was done. I was not allowed to even roam around on deck. The cat patrol officer said this was necessary so that I would not escape on land. Well, I was not happy at all about this. I would never try to escape. Still, there was no way I could explain this to the officer. So, for the next few days I was confined like a prisoner, except during the night, when I had company, because Lee and Sheila were staying down below inside the boat. During the daytime, the boat work that included sandblasting the bottom was extremely noisy, and the air around the boatyard was very dirty. Even though I cried hysterically, no one responded in a positive way.

I was definitely glad when that ordeal was over and the boat was back in the water. Although I never played with the cats on

other boats, I was happy to be back in their company at the marina. I could still enjoy just watching them move about or simply staring at me a short distance away from their places on deck. I have to say that some seemed very attracted to me. One male cat stared for hours with his tongue hanging down. I was not impressed.

Not long after that, it was nearing time for our departure from New Zealand. It was now April (their fall season), and the chance of cyclones up in the tropics south of the equator was diminishing. Eric, another friend of Lee's, arrived from the States to join as crew on the boat for a while. After allowing him some time to rent a car and do some of his own exploring, preparations were made for our departure. Some new equipment was purchased for the boat, and a good supply of provisions were stored below.

At this time of year, sea conditions for our next crossing should be fairly good. However, it was still important to keep an eye on the weather forecast. The next ocean passage would take us up to Fiji, which was about 1,070 miles away back in the tropical zone, and conditions would still be variable until we reached the latitude of the trade winds. Since we had a good radio, we could get daily weather forecasts and keep in radio contact with other yachts sailing in the general area. A good sailor always keeps an eye and ear open for the unexpected.

It was a fine day when we departed, but it still took a few days for me to get my sea legs back. We were now back on the wild blue Southern Ocean and had to re-adapt to the motion of the high seas. However, it was not long before we got used to this previously familiar rhythm, and the days just rolled by as we rolled with them.

CHAPTER 13
Bula Bula in Fiji

Our ocean crossing to Fiji went fairly smoothly without anything remarkable occurring. During the first few days, the weather was variable, as expected. A few mild fronts came through with changes in wind direction between east and west. Still, we were able to keep heading in the right direction, close to our intended rhumb-line (most direct) course. Later, after one day of calm weather, the trade winds came back, and we headed north on a beam reach at a steady pace.

The only significant incident for me happened soon after the trade winds picked up. As we sailed along, I started to notice something unusual while I sat in the cockpit with the rest of the crew. Something was flying through the air close to the surface of the ocean on the crest of each wave. I was quite puzzled until Lee said that it was a school of flying fish. Each of them had fins that looked and acted like wings and that helped them glide for long distances by using drafts of wind that blew over the face of waves. Before I could say anything about it, one of the fish flew right across the deck. A moment later, a fish flew right into my face. More flying fish followed, landing in various locations all over the boat. I wondered if they were blind or just reckless. I guess they didn't realize that our boat was in their flight path until it was too late. I proceeded to lick off the smell of fish on my face and moved around to inspect the other fish as they flopped about on deck. What a sight! I started thinking about our next meal,

but we never did get to eat any. Lee said they were too skinny and didn't taste that good. After removing about ten of these fish from the deck, we sailed on and never saw them again during that crossing.

Although not life threatening, one problem did develop. When we were over halfway to our destination, Lee noticed that the ship's compass wasn't working properly. Upon further inspection, he found that the special fluid that the compass needle floats in had somehow leaked out of the compass. Since we had no other fluid to replace it, the compass became useless for providing the correct heading for steering the boat. After considering his options, Lee decided to use the compass heading provided by the GPS instrument for navigating the rest of the way. It was a good thing we had this piece of equipment, since it served us well.

After about seven days at sea, we spotted the islands of Fiji, and after passing a few, we came to the capital seaport of Suva on the largest central island of Viti Levu. We were now in a part of the Pacific known as Melanesia, where people with ancestries different than the Polynesians lived on clusters of hilly, tropical islands, many surrounded by coral reefs. The watery nation of Fiji, a former member of the British Commonwealth, has a university and a medical school. Although Suva is the largest city in this part of the Pacific, a very tranquil life prevails in the surrounding smaller islands. Our plan was to first check in with customs, get supplies, and then spend a few months visiting the more remote outer islands where life was very peaceful and the people lived in more traditional ways. We never liked to stay in large towns or noisy cities for long.

When we came into Suva, we found a bustling town with lots of foreign cruising yachts and a very good yacht club. While clearing customs and immigration at dockside, the officials asked who else was on the boat. When they heard about me, they came aboard to investigate. When one officer saw me, he was very surprised and wondered if I was a tiger. Well, that was a new one for me. I guess he had never seen a large puss cat. I never thought that I looked that big and ferocious, but I must admit that I often get quite a reaction about my size.

While spending a few days mostly around the yacht club, Lee and the crew went shopping for fresh provisions, got some new fluid for the compass, collected some souvenirs from street vendors, and checked out the cultural scene. They also tried some wonderful curry dishes and pastries provided by Fijians with East-Indian ancestry.

Around that time, an unusual gusty wind, called a bomb storm, came up and quickly moved off to the south. A day later, we heard on the ship's radio that a late-season cyclone had developed in the Southern Ocean from this blow and had intensified as it moved toward New Zealand, crossing paths with a number of yachts. A fleet of cruising yachts that was headed our way were caught in the middle of this storm and had a very rough time. Three of the yachts actually didn't make it, but the people on them were rescued. So sad! I guess we were lucky that we left when we did. Such is the luck or the fate of an ocean sailor. A few days later, some of these wounded yachts came into port, and we heard many terrifying stories.

Soon after that, our temporary crew member Eric flew back home, and Captain Lee made up a route plan for sailing in a loop around the surrounding islands. Once we stocked up on more provisions and a few souvenirs, we departed the port of Suva.

Many of the outer islands we visited had coral reefs around them, so Lee had to climb the ratlines, the rope ladder tied between the mast's rigging wires, and keep a lookout, while Sheila stayed at the helm, taking directions and steering the boat around any shallow coral. This practice is often employed when navigating around tricky waters where shallow reefs are present. Even though I was tempted to climb up and see the view with Lee, I never found the courage. After all, I am primarily a scaredy cat and contrary to stories about sea cats (including me) who love to climb aloft, the rope ladder seemed too difficult for me to use.

Unlike hitting a soft sand bar, running aground on a hard coral reef is no fun. Many yachts have been sunk on such occasions. Sailing in areas with known reefs is one thing, but small, isolated reefs can also be found in what seems to be open ocean. It is wise to keep a watch and stay clear of these reefs, especially since charts may not be that accurate. Lee and Sheila actually had to come to the assistance of one yacht that struck such a reef during the night. When they picked up the distress call on the radio, they spent hours relaying messages to a rescue ship that was out of range of the distress call. In the end, the rescue ship found the yacht and brought the crew and their boat safely into port. Lee and Sheila's assistance in the rescue was later reported

in the local newspaper. I was disappointed that my name was never mentioned.

Fiji is a nation with many traditional ceremonial practices. Visiting cruisers are asked to respect and adhere to some of these traditions, in particular by first offering a gift of kava to the chief of any village they visit. After the chief accepts the kava with a ceremonial speech, the visitors are welcomed to the community and allowed to move around and make friends. As in many other islands in this part of the Pacific, the root of the kava plant is often pounded into a paste, mixed with water, and drunk during social ceremonies. After being informed of this custom in Suva, we stocked up with enough kava to use while visiting the various surrounding islands. Thinking it might be different than before, I again tried some, but still it tasted terrible and made me a bit dizzy. I would never understand why it was so popular.

Making friends with the locals seemed to happen very easily. Those living on the outer islands do not see many tourists, and they treat travelers as honored guests. They have a strong respect for sailors, for they know about the perils of the sea. We were often greeted with "Bula bula," which how Fijians say hello. Although Lee and Sheila made a point of learning certain useful words like this in the native language, for real conversation they often relied on those who did speak English, such as a local school teacher. However, as usual, Lee was still good with his own silly form of sign language, which brought plenty of laughs. The locals were eager for any entertainment we could provide, and we always did our best.

Besides some good trolling for tuna and marlin, as in many tropical islands, the highlight was the great diving on colorful coral reefs where plenty of sea life abounds. Lee and Sheila saw their share of fish along with other sea creatures such as sting rays, moray eels, and sea snakes. Large schools of brightly colored fish—angel fish, tangs, damselfish, wrass, grunts, snapper, butterfly fish, squirrelfish, parrotfish, and triggerfish—would often glide close by or meander about in circles. I often wondered how each got such unique names. Meanwhile, other smaller fish would peek

out from their hiding places in the coral. I think they were likely interested in going to school with the larger fish, but were still too young! But as a cat, I had no way of knowing. The whole scene was like living in another world, and Sheila often brought back some beautiful sea shells to prove it was an underwater paradise. I marveled at the colorful nautilus, cowries, spider conchs, tritons, and trumpet shells that she found.

The island life above water was just as beautiful. Each island had its own natural attractions that brought to life the feeling of paradise. Besides all the colorful flowers amongst the greenery of tropical palm trees and plant life, there were a number of spectacular waterfalls. Since Lee and Sheila went for many hikes during the heat of the day, having waterfalls as the ultimate destination made for a great cooling and refreshing blessing. They also provided a good place to wash their clothes and dry them on nearby rocks. As for me, I was content to simply groom my beautiful fur coat, rub my chin on things, and stay in the shade of the awning on the boat.

Although there were plenty of tropical birds and animal wild-life, it was the domesticated pigs that fascinated Lee the most. He saw a number of enormous female pigs that often had a group of baby piglets staying close by.

It seemed that the largest pigs in all of the South Pacific lived in Fiji. The locals took pride in their pigs and fed them well. I guess the fat ones also tasted better, but I had no way of telling, since they never brought me back a taste. Pigs were often saved for special feasts, where they would be cooked in traditional earth ovens similar to the kind we saw in Tonga.

When it came to human entertainment, there was no short-age. The folks living in small villages were often excited to have foreign visitors, and some families would invite them into their home. Since Lee and Sheila were always curious about their tra-ditional way of life, the local families would share stories about the past, sing songs, perform custom dances, show how they pre-pared local foods, and demonstrate how they made various woven mats, decorative pieces of art, and handicrafts made from plant fiber, sea shells, or wood. Lee and Sheila were even invited to a traditional wedding ceremony where everyone dressed up in colorful outfits.

However, the most unique event they witnessed was a firewalking re-enactment. In the past, firewalking was done as part of a spiritual ceremony. The participants would actually walk barefoot over a bed of hot coals. It seems that they were able to do this by getting into some sort of trance state that prevented them from getting burned by the hot coals. However, this practice had been outlawed by the government and could no longer be performed. When Lee responded with disappointment, one family decided they would present a make-believe demonstration of the ceremony. They made it very entertaining and funny as they sang and giggled while walking over fake hot coals. This all made me wonder what a real trance state would be like. It is probably not

like me being hypnotized by a mysterious moving object like a falling star or meteor.

Another funny thing was the adopted English names that some of the island people used. Since the local people had names that foreigners found difficult to pronounce, some would change their names to those that were well known worldwide. Most often they choose names of famous actors and sports players. Therefore, we got to meet people like "Michael Jordan," "Ringo Starr," and "Marlon Brando." One time, Michael Jordan even came aboard the boat to pat me. They were all fun to be with. I thought about changing my name to the superhero Cat Woman, but decided it wasn't worth it.

Lee and Sheila also met some people who were the offspring of voyaging European seafarers who came here from the distant past. Back in the days of whaling ships, some of the crew would find these islands so inviting that they would jump ship and move in with the locals, much to the dismay of their captains. Over the years, these sailors would adopt the ways of the inhabitants, marry local women, and become an integral part of the island culture. My captain and mate got to know one such family who provided them with a wonderful feast. They held church every Sunday in their house, and we called it the Church of Bob, the father and pastor's name.

On the remote island of Rabi, Lee and Sheila got to visit the local cocoa plantation. They saw some of their fast dugout sailing canoes, watched locals play card games or netball, and made friends with the local school teachers, who spoke good English. One day, Lee was invited to bring his video camera and film the school girls singing traditional songs. It was a very sweet performance. Some were even allowed to come on the boat and visit me. I was very surprised when one of the girls sang a song for me.

We found the cruising life in Fiji to be wonderful as we sailed over short distances from one island paradise to another. It was often hard to move on, because we did not want to keep saying goodbye to our newfound friends. Since there was always too much to see and do, we often stayed longer than planned. However, our destiny was to always continue sailing over the next horizon.

Our most significant visit to a Fijian village was on the remote island of Yadua, where only a few hundred people lived. Since visitors rarely come to their village, they were glad to have us. The island had been previously hit by a bad cyclone, and the local inhabitants had had to struggle putting things back together. It took them quite a while to rebuild the thatched huts in which they lived. With a shortage of good drinking water, natural resources, and government assistance, the locals depended on themselves to survive.

One young man gave a demonstration of the preparation and cooking of sea slugs. An abundant number of these sea cucumbers are found in the local waters. Both Lee and I could not understand why anyone would want to eat these ugly, slimy, rubbery creatures, but it seemed that some people in Asia like them very much. Selling them to East Asian countries provided a much-needed income for the islanders. The only other cash crop was copra, but its value was in decline.

Each day in Yadua was filled with new activity. The headman of the village told us stories about the island's history. One young lady gave a guided tour of the island. The local school also put on a dance performance that Lee filmed with his video camera. Our lives were full of teasing and laughter.

However, the cutest thing I saw from my perch on the boat while it was anchored close to shore was a young boy with a homemade wheelbarrow carrying a baby. I thought this was a very creative way for providing comfort and transportation for a baby in a place with few modern forms of transportation. Why it might even be a good way to transport a cat like me.

After staying for a few weeks, we informed the islanders that we would soon be leaving. Since Lee had filmed lots of videos of the locals and their activities during our stay, many wanted to see themselves on TV. Lee agreed that a few of the them could come out to the boat, where he would show the video scenes on his small TV. Although the people had seen video movies, they had never seen themselves on film and were excited to come.

Well, when that time came, it seems that no one in the village wanted to be left out. As it turned out, a total of forty-four Fijians came out to the boat. This was by far the largest number of visitors we had ever had at one time on our boat. We really had to pack them in down below. Sheila made popcorn, and all the kids wanted to see the famous cat onboard. I was not pleased about that, and after Sheila held me up high and allowed many

of the kids to touch me in various ways, I found a moment where I could escape. Since kids were everywhere on the boat, the only place where I could avoid them was in my kitty litter box. So that is where I stayed hidden for the remainder of time. Even though I could hear everyone laughing while watching themselves on the TV, I was not a happy puss cat.

Over the next week, we sailed westward, making short stops at various anchorages. After anchoring in twenty-seven different locations among the various islands that we visited in Fiji, it was now time to sail on further west. When we arrived at the port of Lautoka on the west side of the big island of Viti Levu, we made preparations for our next ocean crossing. Once we finished shopping for food and provisions, Lee completed our clearance with the Fijian customs and immigrations. After that, we sailed a short distance to our final stop at Musket Cove. Here we found hundreds of cruising yachts, for this was a popular tourist stop. Except for saying hello to a few cruisers we had met before, Lee and Sheila had no interest in this crowded place. After making the boat ready and battening down the hatches, we sailed off to the next cluster of islands in the nation of Vanuatu. We had heard this was a very interesting place to visit and were happy to be moving on.

This downwind crossing with moderate trade winds was a rolly one, but everything went smoothly. Although I never get seasick, I remained in my bunk with my belly rolling back and forth most of the way. The Aries wind vane steered the boat the whole way, and the crew remained fairly relaxed. This self-steering device is great for taking the drudgery out of an ocean passage. It was like having a third mate on board to do all the steering. We covered the distance of about 570 miles in just about four days.

CHAPTER 14

One Bigfella Puss Cat

The country of Vanuatu consists of about thirty-five islands that stretch over many miles from south to north. These islands have high mountains originally formed from volcanoes. As part of the extensive Ring of Fire that circles around the Pacific Ocean, many are still active and erupt periodically. The islanders believe these eruptions are caused through the magic of certain gods, and when you see the glow of fire in a dark night, it's easy to believe that as well.

Numerous different tribes of people inhabit different parts of these islands, separated from each other by high mountain ridges, and over fifty indigenous languages are spoken. When foreign English and French settlers first came here and started vanilla plantations, they found it difficult to communicate with the locals. Therefore, they created a new language so that all those who were hired to work in the plantations could understand one another. This new language, called Bislama, is basically a mix of English, French, and Creole with grammar from traditional languages. It is still spoken as the national language today, and even the country's Parliament debates in Bislama. With a little practice, visitors can learn to understand it. However, regular English is spoken by many, since it is taught in the schools.

Tourism is new to this area, and many locals did not know how to handle foreigners. However, we were usually greeted warmly with much curiosity. The people have kept many of their traditional ways and still perform a variety of custom ceremonies, dances, and rituals. Visitors have to be careful not to interfere with some activities or walk in specific places which are considered taboo or off limits. For the most part, we did not run into any problem with this.

Our first port of entry in Vanuatu was the small capital city of Port Vila on the island of Efate in the southern part of the islands. This is the largest town in a nation of predominantly small villages. After we came alongside the main dock, the customs and immigration officials came aboard. While the paper work was completed, one of the officials who first saw me sitting on the cabin top smiled with eyes open wide. He then spoke of me as being "one bigfella puss cat." This new Bislama name for me sounded quite nice, and I felt so proud that I had to flex my muscles! Lee and Sheila laughed at this. So now you know where my favorite name comes from.

Soon after we moved out to anchor, got rested, and settled in, Lee and Sheila went out to explore the town. As for this fella, I

was content to lie on deck and watch nearby bird life along the shore. That evening, when Lee and Sheila returned, they mentioned that an Australian company was making a movie about Vanuatu. Lee said they had even been asked to be a part of it by acting as tourists. Now this was unusual to say the least. But over the following days, they and some other cruisers spent a fair amount of time acting with the group. I would have loved to see them make fools of themselves, but as usual I could not venture ashore.

However, one day there was a special custom dance in plain view on shore not far away from me. A group of native dancers were practicing a tourist welcome song for one of the movie scenes. It was performed in a traditional way with dancers decorated with flowers on their heads, while singing and dancing around in a circle. I got to have a front row seat for the spectacle and soon made a few twists and turns of my own while wiggling my butt.

The main actors were from the One Small Bag Theater, which got its name from the saying "Good things...come in small packages" or "...i kam long wan smol bag" in Bislama. The movie portrayed how the first arrival of tourists affected life in a small village of tribal people. The results were shown to be both good and bad for the locals. Lee and Sheila and all the other actors had a great time and got to learn a lot about the local customs and traditions of Vanuatu.

When the production was over, all participants were invited to a big party where kava was consumed. It turns out that in Vanuatu there are many varieties of kava, and some are quite strong. Each morning, it was very common to see many men laying around being quite lazy. Lee had more than his fill and slept in late. Sheila just drank Pepsi, so she was fine the next day.

On another occasion, a boy came down to the town pier and made some music with an unusual green plant held between his teeth. I am not sure how he was able to do that, but he made some very odd sounds that you could hear over a long distance. The sound was very different from blowing a conch shell and had a much higher pitch. It seemed to sound like a bird who was singing with a sore throat.

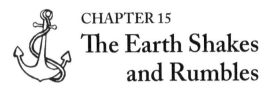

CHAPTER 15

The Earth Shakes and Rumbles

After a few more fun days playing around in Port Vila, we headed south along with another yacht toward the island of Tanna. In the center of this island is Mount Yasur, an active volcano that makes Tanna a popular place for cruisers to visit. Along the way, we stopped each evening at an anchorage, since Lee did not feel like sailing at night. On the day before arriving at Tanna, we sailed by a spot where the water actually bubbled up at the surface due to some underwater volcanic activity. We had never seen this before. Since we did not know what might happen, we kept our distance.

The next day, we heard on the radio that there was a tsunami (giant wave) warning due to an earthquake that occurred somewhere in the area. The announcer said that the boats anchored in Port Resolution, the primary harbor at the island of Tanna, should leave until the threat was over. All the boats but one headed out to deep water, where a tidal wave would not be a problem. I'm not sure why the foolish captain on the one boat stayed behind. At the time, we were still hours away from the harbor, but we still proceeded with caution.

Although there was no real danger for us, we did experience a momentary shudder as some nearby underwater earthquake rattled the rigging and shook the boat. When it happened, I felt like I had turned into a vibrating cat and feared my tail would fall off. The shuddering lasted for about ten minutes, and after it ended, I

was still quivering. This was the first time Lee had experienced an earthquake while sailing at sea. Since we were in deep water, no harm was done to us or the boat.

Not long afterward, the announcer on the radio reported that the threat had passed, and all the yachts returned to Port Resolution. Meanwhile, we continued on and arrived there a few hours later. We found the harbor full of cruising yachts with a nice little village on a nearby coastal hill. After meeting with some yachties (another name for cruisers) and visiting the local chief of the village, Lee and Sheila explored the village and spent some time practicing how to speak Bislama. Lee had a fine time ashore playing with some local kids, while I rested happily on the boat. I later heard he also taught the kids how to do some yoga.

We soon found out about a unique group of people that lived not far away in another village. These locals were part of the John Frum cargo cult. It originated during World War II when the first American soldiers parachuted onto the island. At that time, the primitive tribal people had never seen a plane and were amazed when people and large parcels of mostly canned food dropped from the sky onto the land. Later, they met one soldier who was called John. They were very curious and asked John where he came from. Hence the name "John Frum" was created. They treated John and the others that had descended out of the sky as gods and have since wondered when they might magically return with more gifts. As odd as this sounds, it is true. The cult that developed since then still prays for them to return and carries on with some unusual ceremonies to this day. Many of the cruisers went to visit their village and watch their musical dance performances.

However, the primary attraction on Tanna is the active volcano Mount Yasur. Although tourism was relatively new here, the locals had the good sense to organize trips to the volcano for a reasonable fee, which helped bring some income to the community. Since the volcano was a very unusual attraction for travelers,

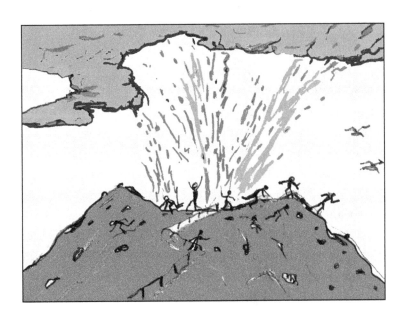

anyone that came here would not pass up the chance to see it. After riding in a jeep to a location part way up the mountain, all the visitors had to climb on foot to the rim of the volcano.

Now this would have never been allowed in most other place around the world, for it was very dangerous to be that close to an active volcano. Still, the locals and the visitors didn't think much about that. When they arrived at the rim of the half-mile-wide crater at the top, they could stand on the edge and look down inside. There they saw repetitive bursts of fiery hot lava erupting from far below, continually arising from different locations within the crater. Lee and Sheila were amazed at this powerful spectacle.

Although many may not have thought about any possible danger, they were there at their own risk. There were no safety lines, and when each burst of molten lava exploded, many of those watching felt the need to jump back. Makes sense to me. Although most of the explosions were at a fair distance from the onlookers, we later heard that some fireballs had not only come close to some visitors, but had killed one Japanese tourist. Sometimes, ignorance is not bliss.

Other kinds of shaking and rumbling came mostly from musical vibrations provided by the islanders. A number of dance bands had been formed over the years, especially string bands, in which guitars, rattles, bottles, and a washtub bass were used in the performance. Some of the music they played was traditional, and some more recent. Lee met one group that wanted him to make a video of their performance. It turned out to be quite comical, for they wanted to perform each song at a different natural location. They would sometimes play by a campfire or a river. However, the most unusual place was on top of a rock that sat out in the shallow water just offshore close to where we were anchored. It was not very easy for them to climb up and get ready, but that did not stop them. Since I like music, it was good entertainment for soothing my savage soul.

Another common sight was young boys beating on split-log drums of various sizes. Each of the logs had a different tone, and

each of the boys kept their own rhythm in tune with the others. Since the boat was anchored close enough to shore, I was often able to hear them. They beat on the log drums for hours with only short breaks to laugh at something funny. It was probably because Lee was doing something silly. I can still hear the laughing and drumming in my sleep.

Lee and Sheila also got to see another band that provided a unique performance. This band dressed up in traditional native costume and danced while playing a variety of musical instruments. One of the performers made a sweet tinkling sound by tapping a stick on a collection of different-sized bottles filled partially with water. Other members of the group used guitars and a variety of rattles. Some of the dancers moved spears around in motion with the music. It was a very impressive performance.

After leaving the island of Tanna, we slowly made our way north stopping each day at a new island anchorage. Both the local waters and the tropical jungles on each island had something different to offer. At each stop, we found something unique and enjoyable, but our encounters with animals and wildlife was not always pleasant. 🐾

CHAPTER 16

Bad Bugs and
Other Creatures

At one of the stops amongst the islands of Vanuatu, the locals told us about a friendly manatee, which is large aquatic mammal also called a dugong. This type of sea creature looks like a fat baby whale and likes to hang out in shallow inlets. They are generally considered harmless and have been known to be friendly to humans. The natives said this one even liked to be touched and would often cuddle up with a person while they were swimming together.

Since this sounded quite interesting, a female friend from another cruising boat decided to go and play with the dugong. When she got in the water and swam close by, the dugong seemed to respond in a positive way. However, when she dove under him, the friendly dugong pressed himself down on top of her. Although it was likely a friendly gesture, it prevented her from coming up for air. She soon became frightened and struggled to get free. Finally, she did, and swam quickly to the surface. That was being too friendly for her liking. If there was a next time, she would know to stay on top while being embraced.

Many of our anchorages in the bays and coves around these islands had wonderful beaches with black sand created by the erosion of volcanic rocks along the shore. Since these anchorages were well protected from the ocean swell, landing by dinghy was easy and often accomplished without any problem. However, on one occasion when Lee and Sheila landed, they encountered a

very unexpected intrusion from the local insects. Small bugs are rarely a problem when anchored further offshore where a breeze keeps them away, but they love to hang out on shore, especially around sunset.

However, this time it was just around noon, so they were quite surprised when an army of sand flies, horseflies, mosquitos and some other unknown species attacked them. As much as they wanted to explore the island, there was no way they could handle the swarm of insects. They quickly rowed back to the boat. I had to be sympathetic when I saw Sheila with all her bug bites. I was glad our boat was anchored far enough away from shore to keep me safe, for I have always detested invasive insects.

We did hear stories about larger wild animals such as tigers and even bears, but we never had a threatening encounter with them. Traveling in the tropics does have its problems like these, and if you lived there for any length of time, you would have to learn the best way to handle or avoid them.

Even though I stayed on the boat, I had my own share of animal encounters. Most often they involved either birds or fish. These experiences were never dangerous or life threatening, but rather quite fun and entertaining for me. However, sometimes my encounter with the birds was just frustrating, since it was difficult to get close enough to catch one. Keep in mind, I am not mean, and my attraction to birds or anything that flies about is just part of my natural instinct.

It was around this time that a sea bird came and landed on the deck railing. My eyes quickly spotted this bird, and I slyly moved closer. The bird seemed to care little about me and just ruffled his feathers and proceeded to clean himself. When I got close enough, I pretended not to be looking. Then I turned quickly and thrust my paw in his direction. The bird took a short hop further down the rail. I continued to pursue him and was amazed at his fearlessness. It turned out to be the longest time for me to have a bird that close, and I could not help staying in pursuit. Still, the bird just kept moving to different locations all over the boat. Lee and Sheila were very entertained by my frustrated attempts to catch up with the bird.

Although Lee and Sheila would sometimes find old bones from whales or other wild animals, it was the bones treasured by a local chief that intrigued them the most. A large collection of the tusks of wild boars, commonly eaten only on special occasions such as weddings or funerals, signifies great status. So, when Lee met one island chief with many tusks on display, he knew he was with a very respected individual of high rank in the village. The chief was very happy to show them off.

As we sailed along through these islands, we got to see more active volcanoes, though we never ventured as close as before. Sometimes when anchored at night, we could see a red glow rising out of them. Meanwhile, most of the jungle we explored had wonderful scenery that was very lush and green. When on hikes over land, Lee and Sheila also saw a number of old plantations and villages with traditional wooden totem statues with faces carved into them. On Pentecost Island, they discovered the

location where bungee jumping originated. As part of a fertility ritual, tribal warriors would show their bravery by jumping off a manmade tower and descending head first. The vine attached to their ankles stopped stretching just before they hit the ground. I often wonder how many of them miscalculated and were killed upon landing.

One other thing that was fascinating to me was how many of the local tribal people thanked Lee for saving them from the Japanese during World War II. Why Lee was not even born then! Still, the locals liked to keep stories from the past alive and told them as if they had just occurred yesterday. In this case, it seemed that they were very glad when the American army did come and freed them from the torturous grasp of the invading Japanese army. There are also a number of locations where you can find large shipwrecks of war ships from that time. These wrecks have become popular sites for divers, since many are located close to the surface of the shallow water.

As time passed and our voyage took us further north, we came closer to our final stops in the islands of Vanuatu. It was also nearing the time that cyclones would start occurring in the South Pacific. Therefore, we needed to cross over to the north of the equator to avoid them. However, there is no exact time when this transition occurs. It is just an approximate time period when cyclones end to the north of the equator and begin to the south of the equator.

As it turned out, an early cyclone had developed to the south, and we needed to find a good hurricane hole to anchor in until it passed. Luckily, we found an ideal place at one of the most northern islands in Vanuatu. While securely anchored there, we did get some strong winds, but the eye of the storm soon moved away from our location. It was now time to move on to the Banks Islands located closer to the equator.

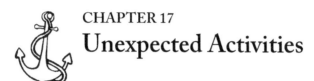

CHAPTER 17

Unexpected Activities

After an overnight sail, we arrived at the Banks Islands. This little group of small, hilly islands was to be the last ones we visited before making another long ocean crossing up to Micronesia in the North Pacific Ocean.

Upon arrival at our first island anchorage, the local chief came out in his small canoe from the nearby village. He wanted to know if we had any batteries for his radio. Luckily, we had some, and when we gave them to him, his face lit up with a big smile. These islands are far from any real civilization, and having radio contact with the rest of the world is important for the local inhabitants. Since very few yachts come here, they have little chance to trade. The next morning, he brought us a gift of some local fresh fruit and fish. Now you're talking!

At the next island, we stopped at Lakona Bay, where we were also greeted warmly. Chief Johnstar took Lee on a tour of the village and a hike into the jungle bush. During the following days, Lee traded fish hooks for more fresh fruit, and the local teacher gave a tour of his small school house. Many of the children followed Sheila, for they were fascinated with her long, red, wavy hair. One girl spent hours combing Sheila's hair while all the other children watched and giggled. What a silly bunch!

Everyone on the island seemed to be content living a very simple life. Most of the kids were happy playing easy games, and one particular game was quite unique. A group of singing kids gathered together in the center, while another group paraded around them in a circle. Those in the outer circle were dressed up in all sorts of green plants. Each of them pretended to be hiding a coconut while the group in the center had to guess which one really had the coconut. It was fun to watch, and even some very young children joined in the fun. But one baby cried when he saw Lee. He was probably scared by the unusual appearance of his white skin and beard. That night I dreamed that I was part of the fun, but had difficulty hiding a large coconut under my fur.

The island has awesome scenery and is very lush with plant life. There is plenty of fresh food for everyone, and after a harvest, you would see the women heading home carrying bundles of fruits and veggies on their heads. Fish were plentiful, and each family had their own canoe. Children spent a lot of time playing in the water, and babies learned to feel secure in the warm, shallow waters at an early age. Definitely not something I would admire or wish for, but I realized it was natural for them.

The elders were well respected and cared for by the community, and each village had a small school house. Although only one island had a clinic, most of the islanders seemed fairly healthy. Even if they had some health issues, they still kept their sense of humor, and not a day would pass without some laughter.

Since supply ships seldom come to the island, people had learned to live without certain store-bought provisions. Some of the inhabitants also seemed to have some magical skills. We heard stories about special rituals that help prevent the locals from being harmed by bad spirits. Whether you believe in this kind of thing or not, the islanders seemed reassured by the presence of those with special healing powers.

Since Lee had a video camera, many of the locals wanted some of their special activities to be filmed. One particular performance that I was able to see from my spot on the boat was quite unusual. In fact, this is one of the few places in the world where it's done. This activity may have come from a practice used to attract fish.

Most fish are known to be attracted to the sound of splashing on the surface of the water, because they think there are fish in trouble and vulnerable to attack. They often hurry to the location of the noise with the idea that they will find food. When some fishermen realized this, they took on the practice of splashing the water as a way to attract fish for dinner. Over time, the practice became modified into a fun activity. Even though I can appreciate their intentions, it is not a practice that I would ever attempt to do.

On this island, the local women had made it into a musical performance. A line of women would stand waist deep in the shallow waters by the beach and repeatedly slap the water with their hands to make a drumming sound. Each water drummer had her own rhythm, and all together it made for a powerful song. Both Lee and I watched them with fascination. At one point, the women refused to continue unless Lee danced on the beach to the rhythm of their water drumming. When he consented to wiggle his butt and jump around, all the women let out a loud

roar of laugher. Now that really made me smile and laugh inside. You probably know I cannot laugh out loud since I'm a cat.

We were having so much fun at this island that we ended up staying for about a week. During that time, we invited many of our new friends out for cake and tea. I received lots of attention and got many good pats that made me purr for a long time. Sheila also provided radio contact with some of the people's relatives on other islands. Meanwhile, Lee had fun playing games with the kids and trading gifts. We were lucky that English was taught in the local school, for it made communication much easier.

Before leaving, we told Chief Johnstar about our plan to sail far north to the islands of Micronesia. He knew about the cyclones in the area and recommended that we have some magic performed by a local healer as a form of protection. He said that it would help keep us free from bad storms. Although Lee was skeptical about this, he agreed. Later that day, Lee and Sheila met with the magic man, and he performed the ritual. Although it did not seem to amount to much, Lee prayed that it would work and thanked him. However, looking back, I can now say that even though we did not encounter the ultimate bad cyclone, the long ocean crossing to Micronesia was a rough and messy one.

Soon after this, we loaded up with more fresh produce, waved goodbye to our new friends, and sailed up to the next island, which was uninhabited. When we came close to shore, we found a splendid anchorage where two waterfalls cascaded down close to shore. Lee and Sheila had a very refreshing time swimming while I watched them from the boat and took a few sips from my water bowl.

The next day, we sailed up to the small island of Motu Lava. Since this was our last stop before the next long crossing, Lee and Sheila spent the day getting the boat ready and loading on extra fresh fruit. The dinghy was secured on deck, and all the boat's equipment was stowed below. The last of the fresh kitty litter was put in my cat box. It was now time to sail over many sea miles across the equator to the islands of Micronesia in the North Pacific.

PART 3

Through Micronesia
to the Land of Oz

CHAPTER 18

The Worst Crossing Ever

As I previously mentioned, it was now the time of year when the cyclone season ends in the North Pacific and starts up in the South Pacific. However, the western part of the North Pacific often has a longer season with more cyclones than any other ocean in the world. For this reason, we would have to be careful and listen to all the weather reports on our single-sideband (SSB) marine radio. This very useful type of short-wave radio can receive messages from hundreds of miles away.

In addition, the area close to both sides of the equator is what's called a tropical convergence zone, where the prevailing trade-wind patterns below and above the equator mix in a zone of unpredictability Weather conditions would be variable with plenty of shifting winds, squalls, calm spells, and swirling countercurrents. Therefore, our progress would be slow until we got far enough north to reach the North Pacific trade winds. But when we got close to that location in latitude, we would then be in the area where cyclones could still develop. Since the total distance to our next island destination was over a thousand miles away, we were likely to have our hands full. I was hopeful that didn't include my paws, except if they were holding my food bowl.

In many parts of the world, crossing the equator is not that much of a problem, for there are no storms that last very long. Usually there are mostly light winds, which require sailors to run the motor to pass through the area. However, in the western

Pacific Ocean, other factors related to strong monsoon winds from East Asia can have an influence, so standing watch to look for any changes in cloud formations that signal changes in wind strength and direction is important. Any changes in wind could require a change of sails, but nobody could easily predict exactly what would happen ahead of time. As it turned out, we had the longest and most difficult sea crossing of our voyage, which we later called "The Crossing from Hell." Definitely not a time that I remember fondly.

On the day of our departure, I am happy to say that we were greeted by a group of dolphins. They splashed around for almost an hour. It made for a splendid send off, and I was truly fascinated. As we cleared the north end of Motu Lava, we found a pleasant easterly trade wind breeze that allowed us to easily hold our intended course to the north. For the next few days, the sailing was good.

However, as we got closer to the equator, conditions changed, and winds became light and variable. Lee was not surprised, as this was expected. Before long, our progress became much slower, and billowing cumulus clouds often appeared, bringing shifting, gusty winds. The seas became lumpy and confused with small waves coming from different directions. It was necessary to use the motor for a few hours each day during the calm spells. I spent my time hiding out in a quiet, cozy spot down below in the bow.

At night, the stars were bright, and one night we saw a moon bow, which is like a rainbow that forms when reflected particles of moisture create a distinct band of colors through the sunlight in the sky. Except this time, it was the light of the moon that created it. Lee said this was a rare phenomenon that he had only seen once before.

Later on, the abundance of large clouds that appeared during the night not only obscured our ability to see any stars, but made

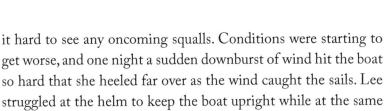

it hard to see any oncoming squalls. Conditions were starting to get worse, and one night a sudden downburst of wind hit the boat so hard that she heeled far over as the wind caught the sails. Lee struggled at the helm to keep the boat upright while at the same time adjusting the sails as lightning arrived with a downpour of rain. This was the beginning of more drama to come. A period of time when I was unable to purr.

During the daytime, it was definitely easier to see any dark bands of clouds coming so that we could change sails in time to handle the strong winds that came with the clouds. Since Lee was the most experienced sailor, it was often his job to handle the hardest work on the boat. As the days passed, he became more and more tired due to lack of sleep. He eventually found out that just getting a short "cat nap" would help give him enough energy to keep on doing his job. Meanwhile, my cat naps lasted much longer, as I remained mostly inactive down below in the most secure location I could find.

For the next few days, we experienced a mix of heavy rains, monsoon squalls, adverse wind shifts, calm spells, lightning, and encounters with many black bands of clouds as we sailed on often-lumpy seas. In addition, we had developed a problem with the motor that made it hard to start. Seems there was some kind of air leak in the fuel line. One night we couldn't get it to start as we were drifting without any wind toward an approaching fishing boat. After we flashed our lights, the boat finally moved out of our way. Our course became even more erratic as we continued across the equator.

It was about two days later that the wind dropped completely, and we drifted aimlessly in the calm seas. Lee did get the motor running again, but after it was on long enough to charge the ship's batteries, he turned it off. A while later, very strong winds came up, forcing Lee to hoist the heavy storm sails. It was a good thing he did, because the winds soon increased to 50 knots with the waves rising high. Lee thought this was a bit odd, but when Sheila heard the radio report about a developing cyclone, she found the answer. When comparing the radio report with our own location, we learned that we had been sailing in the calm eye of a developing cyclone. When the eye of this hurricane moved on past us, we became caught in the storm winds that circle around the central eye. In a way, we were lucky to be there when it was a baby cyclone, for when the cyclone moved further north, it became stronger, with winds over 120 knots. That means the same as about 140 miles per hour! In the end, we were able to ride out the storm without further incident, though a freighter we spoke with on the radio was having a rough time in a location further to the north, where the winds were even stronger.

Eventually, we made it far enough north in latitude to reach the trade winds. During our last few days at sea, conditions improved. Even though Lee was still tired from handling the boat

through all the changing sea conditions, he now felt better knowing we would soon be arriving at our destination. I was also looking forward to it, since my belly was tired of rolling about in the rough seas. But little did Lee know it would still be a while before he would have a good night's sleep.

On the morning of our eighteenth day at sea, we finally spotted the island of Kosrae, which was to be our first stop in Micronesia. When we got closer, Lee tried to see if the engine would start, since we would likely need it to maneuver through the pass into the harbor. He had no luck, and after a few attempts, he gave up. He decided that we would have to attempt to sail in while keeping the anchor ready.

Knowing that this would be a bit tricky since the wind might drop inside the pass, Lee got on the radio and called for anyone who might give assistance. Luckily, there was one cruising yacht in the harbor, and they agreed to come out in their motorized dinghy. Sure enough, just as we were carefully watching our drift while entering the pass close to a reef, the wind did drop. Our new friends with the dinghy arrived just in time and slowly pushed our boat into the inner cove, thereby avoiding the reefs. Then they showed us where they thought would be a good place to anchor. Once inside the wide cove, we were able to catch enough wind to sail to that location and drop the anchor. For the moment, we were most relieved, and I stretched out to rest my aching bones next to Sheila, while she relaxed on a bunk down below.

After sharing warm greetings with the cruisers and being informed that, since it was Sunday, customs would not come to clear the boat until the next day, Lee and Sheila fell asleep. However, their rest was short lived. The crew on the other boat did not really know the depth of the water or the extent of the tide in the cove where we had dropped anchor. In addition, our anchor was not dug in well. Later that night, our boat drifted onto a

shallow mud bank as it swung on the changing tide and the anchor slipped along the surface of the bottom. When dawn came, Lee and Sheila found our boat sitting high and dry on its side, resting on the mud bank. It was a rude occasion for me, because I was awakened from my deep sleep by falling out of my bunk.

When the customs agents came out later on to do their paperwork, they had difficulty climbing up on the boat. They told us not to worry and to just come in to their office after getting the boat properly anchored in deeper water. When the tide rose and we got free, Lee finally got the motor running, and we were able to re-anchor in a better location. Now maybe Lee could get more rest. But he was too tired to sleep and spent the day organizing the boat and going to shore to complete the customs clearance and get some fresh food at the nearby store. After that, we did get a good night sleep. However, I still felt quite unsettled and spent the night walking around the deck expecting something more dramatic to happen. As it turned out, my sixth sense was right, for I did not have to wait long for more excitement.

Sheila had been keeping track of radio reports about another late-season cyclone that was developing some distance to the east of the island. The next day, while Lee had gone ashore, the radio reported that the storm was now quickly moving toward the island. She became very anxious, and I could do little to console her. When the winds did increase, she became very worried and sent one of our new cruiser friends ashore to tell Lee to return. But before Lee arrived, the winds quickly got up to gale strength with gusts blowing down off the nearby mountain. She was almost in tears when Lee finally returned.

Lee soon realized that the boat was again dragging anchor over the slippery mud bottom and slowly drifting to the nearby shore. He quickly gave Sheila a hug and then prepared to set a stronger storm anchor to hold the boat in place. It was a bit tricky to accomplish this in the gusty winds. However, once he had the outboard motor mounted on the dinghy and set the new anchor out in the best location, the boat stopped drifting to shore. He also put out a third anchor just in case. Sheila, Lee, and I now felt relieved.

For the next few hours, the winds increased, with gusts up to seventy knots. Tin roofs flew off the nearby houses in the village, and many locals ran for shelter. Although the eye of the storm did not pass that close to the island, there was plenty of damage to the village.

An odd thing during all this time was the activity at a church located nearby on the shore. Since it was the month of December and close to the Christmas holiday, a number of locals were practicing Christmas carols in the church during all the high winds. While our boat was dragging anchor and drifting in the direction of the church, some of the people had wandered outside to watch us. They didn't seem to be bothered by the situation, but maybe they were a little concerned.

Well, I am happy to say that by the end of that day, the winds had settled down, and life was finally back to normal. Whatever that means! The rest of our stay was pleasant enough, with plenty of sleep for all of us each night. I could now purr with contentment more often.

During the remainder of our stay, as was often the case, Lee and Sheila made many friends. They shared meals with some local

families and explored different parts of the island. These Micro-nesian natives had more possessions and modern conveniences that many other Pacific Ocean islanders. After being invaded by the Japanese during World War II, they had become part of the Trust Territory of the Pacific, a confederation administered by the U.S.A. The island even had its own airport. Travelers like us were not as much of a novelty as we had previously been in more remote locations.

For the rest of our stay, we got to enjoy all the parades and singing performances that were part of the Christmas celebra-tion. They even had a Santa Claus that came down in a pickup truck to bring gifts for the children. Afterwards, there was an all-you-can-eat feast. Our stay lasted about three weeks, and when we departed, we had the company of another cruising yacht to sail along westward with us to the next island of Pohnpei.

CHAPTER 19

Finding Our Favorite Paradise

The two-and-half-day ocean crossing, covering about 375 miles to the island of Pohnpei, went fairly smoothly. Since we were now well into the winter season, we had no more cyclones to contend with. Having another cruising yacht to sail along with made for a rare and delightful change. Since they moved along at about the same speed, they were close by most of the way.

During that time at sea, Lee made several attempts to catch some fish. The first time he caught one, a bigger fish got to it first. When he pulled it in, all that was left was a fish head. The next time, he caught a large wahoo, but after a long struggle trying to bring it in, the fish somehow got away. I was very disappointed for I longed to taste a fish with that name. I really wanted to say "Yahoo, I got a wahoo." Lee said it was the next-best-eating fish to swordfish, which was one of his favorites.

The island of Pohnpei is the principal island in the Federated States of Micronesia, an island group that is spread out over many miles. This is where the capital town is located, and it's a good place to get mail from back home because of its connections to the U.S. We ended up staying there for about a month, partly because we needed to wait for a shipment of boat parts and also to get our visas for our planned visit to Australia in the future.

The main seaport was fairly modern, and a moderate number of cruisers were moored close to a small yacht club. Lee and Sheila made a number of new friends, went on hikes around the island, swam at waterfalls, and climbed hilltops with grand views. One of the primary sites of interest on the island was the huge Japanese fort with hidden caves left behind from World War II. The story is that some Japanese soldiers hid out there for months after the war was over.

However, the most significant ruins were those at Nan Madol. They were built centuries before by the native inhabitants of that time. The extent of the remaining stone structures, now entwined with roots and other overgrowth, reveals the amazing ability of those early people. It has a number of stone pyramids enclosed within high walls and hand-hewn canals. How they built such a place is definitely a mystery. One theory is that the structures were built by giants, for the stones are far too big for humans to have handled.

As for my time in Pohnpei, I must say that there were some new encounters worth mentioning. Two of the cruising sailboats close by us in the anchorage had cats. On one boat, there was a male cat named Squish. Since he would often stare at me from his boat, his owner felt it would be good for him to make a visit. When I saw Squish being rowed over in their dinghy, I immediately had my doubts. For one thing, what kind of name is Squish? He looked as if his face was squished in. Maybe he had been squeezed into some small compartment on the boat. Anyway, I had no say in the matter and soon found him staring at me from one end of my boat. I felt it was only natural to hiss and arch my back to look larger while standing my ground. It seems this did keep him from coming any closer, and after a while his owner took him back home.

Now if that were not enough, it seems the captain of another boat in the anchorage wanted his cat Cookie to also make a visit. Now I presume this cat loves to eat cookies, but I may be wrong. In any case, on the very next day I found myself confronted with

this female puss after she was deposited directly in front of me in the cockpit of the boat. Well, even though her face was much nicer, I was still not very interested, and I did not want to share my boat with another cat. In time, after the crew had a few laughs, she was removed from my boat. I have since wondered if she made it around the world to become a global sea cat like me.

That is enough about me, for Lee was now getting excited about something else. He had found that in one part of the town there was a separate village that had a number of indigenous folks from the island of Kapingamarangi. What a mouthful! The men are very talented and make wonderful carvings out of wood and ivory nut. They sell their works of art to tourists as a way to help bring in an income that they send to the families living back on their remote island home. Since the name of that island is very long, everybody uses the shorter name of Kapinga. It's like that even on their baseball caps.

Lee had previously heard about the island, and since it was along our intended cruising route back south, he definitely planned to stop there. The island is over 350 miles away and supply ships few and far between, so while in Pohnpei, he made a point of offering to carry much-needed provisions and mail to those living on Kapinga. Lee was happy to do this, and loaded our boat with rice, beans, flour, and other dry goods. They would arrive with us long before a supply ship would make it there.

After completing some final chores and loading the boat with some new equipment and more provisions, we headed out of the harbor and set sail for Kapinga. For the first day, we had fair winds and following seas. We made only one short, overnight stop along the way at another island. The weather for the remainder of the trip was mostly fine with light winds as we sailed southwest back closer to the equator. We arrived at Kapinga about three days later. As things turned out, this was to be our favorite island paradise during all six years of cruising around the world.

The atoll island of Kapingamarangi is located about sixty miles north of the equator and consists of a circle of low-lying atoll islands that surround a beautiful inner lagoon. Only about 400 people live on two of the small islands. These people are Polynesians who migrated here many, many years ago from the eastern part of the Pacific Ocean. Sailing in their traditional outrigger canoes and guided by the stars and currents, they covered thousands of miles to find their new home. Although during the last century they have been influenced by modern society, they still retain many of their traditional ways and practices, along with their Polynesian language. When we said that the far-distant Easter Island was called Te Pito o Te Henua, they knew it meant "navel of the universe." Well, you could have fooled me, for my navel is not the center of the universe.

When we arrived through the passage on the south side and found our way over the inner lagoon to the village, we were immediately struck by the beauty of this island paradise. The turquoise lagoon waters were very clear, and all the underwater sea life was plainly visible. The main island is about one mile long with a smooth, silvery sand beach extending along the inner shore. Traditional thatched huts were scattered among palm trees throughout the island and connected only by a footpath. A taro patch and various small gardens were located in the center of the island. No vehicles or roads here.

Although one other yacht did stop for a short visit to the island, there were no other foreign visitors during our six-week stay. In fact, very few cruisers come this way. When Lee went ashore to meet the chief and told him that we brought mail and produce, we were greeted warmly. Practically every morning after that, someone would bring a gift of fresh-caught fish to our boat. What more could a cat want! This was definitely my favorite paradise.

Our arrival was very timely, since a week-long "thanksgiving festival" celebration was soon to begin. The festival was in honor of a taro garden that had been created years before in the center of the island. The local inhabitants were very creative and fun loving and knew how to survive with what simple things they possessed. Everyone lived as if they were one big family, sharing and helping anyone in need. Although they had some modern conveniences, they were not dependent on them. If they ran out of fuel for a fishing boat's engine, they would just use their sailing canoes. They might have an aluminum cooking pot, but they would likely use a leaf for a spoon.

These islanders were used to being isolated from the rest of the world, and over the years had learned how to get along. Many who had gone away for a while returned to the island to be with their family and live the good life. The locals who had sampled the modern world still preferred their older, simpler way of life. Everyone seemed to realize that survival was a matter of community cooperation. Their ancestors sailed on long voyages between distant islands, and they knew how to preserve food for those trips. They even knew how to make a dry candy from breadfruit and—believe it or not!—ice cream from coconut milk. Now that is quite tasty!

I was so glad to have some new treats for my limited diet. I would never have to worry about getting scurvy, a dreaded disease caused by lack of proper nutrition that plagued sailors in the distant past who stayed away at sea too long without a good diet.

When the first local visitors came out to the boat, I was treated as royalty, and the kids called me "puti taman." Another new name to add to my collection. Most of the kids were gentle when patting me, so I did not need to run away. Whenever I sat in plain view on the boat, some kids would swim over for a closer look. One time, I saw a very large group hanging on to the dinghy while they whistled to me. I just sat on the deck licking my fur and pretending to ignore them. Actually, I was quite pleased to be held in such high regard.

Except for the small babies who swung in their hammocks in the shade, most of the children and adults seemed to spend a lot of time swimming and playing in the water. Some of the locals even ate their meals while sitting waist deep in the lagoon. It makes perfect sense when you consider how warm it is near the equator. However, the heat is not that unbearable, for there is often a nice sea breeze.

Besides making some great new friends (as it seems we often do), the highlight of our visit was the local festival celebration. Each day, events started with a boy blowing a conch shell. This was followed by lots of traditional songs and dances. Next, there would be some theatrical performances with lots of funny clowns acting out some story while dressed in a variety of comical or traditional costumes. Every day there would be a different kind of entertainment. There was even a doughnut-eating contest where participants had to try and eat doughnuts hanging on a string without using their hands. In addition, there were foot races on

land and canoe or swimming races on the water. I really enjoyed the sleek sailing canoe races the most. They often came close by the boat where they would smile and wave to me on deck.

Each day, the various activities were concluded with a grand feast where food was served to everyone on the island. Dishes often included a fish stew or chowder, bowls of rice, breadfruit, taro, bananas, papaya, and a variety of other fruits, followed with doughnuts and coconut ice cream for dessert. However, the favorite dish for this occasion was moray eel. An abundant number of these eels live in the surrounding reefs, and the local fishermen spent days catching them with homemade traps. When the traps were full, they were brought back to land, where the eels were prepared and cooked slowly overnight for the grand feast on the following day. The whole process requires great care, for the eels have sharp teeth and a strong bite that will not let go. Although we were not that excited about their greasy taste, the locals seemed to love eating them.

After the festival was over, Lee and Sheila had plenty of time to explore the island and make more new friends. Besides the more recent interest in bingo and volleyball, most of the locals took pleasure in very simple activities like playing marbles or card games. Sheila invited a number of the local women to visit our boat and have some of her homemade cake and tea. One old man loved to come out and have coffee and crackers. He was a great story teller. The young boys would often come to hear some good music on our tape player and play with me. Lee spent much of his time on shore and even got to play some ping pong (sadly without me) with the young boys. Lee visited many of the local craftsman to see their wonderful ivory nut carvings, homemade net traps, and decorative handicrafts made from local plants. He had a wonderful time watching some men form a dugout canoe from a breadfruit tree log.

Lee also got to take part in the building of a new home for one of the locals. Any time someone needs help fixing a boat or building a traditional thatched hut with a roof made of pandanus leaves, many people come to help. The sharing of the work load is a tradition here, so no one has to carry the burden alone. With all this help, these traditional homes can be built in a single day and will last for many years. When it is finished, there is a ritual blessing followed by a feast for all the help.

As the weeks passed by, we knew that we would be leaving soon. It was going to be very hard for us, since we had come to love the island and its people. But before it was time to go, we had one last wonderful experience. The old man who often came to the boat for coffee and crackers had two granddaughters around the age of three or four. One day while we were sitting around on the beach, he decided to have them perform a traditional dance for us. It seems that children are taught these dances at a very young age and even though they are not very skilled at it, they can perform the basic moves. So as grandpa sang each song, they

made their bodies move and sway to the music. It was very cute. Meanwhile, I strode around on deck wiggling my butt as the sound of the songs tickled my whiskers.

When the day of our departure was close at hand, one of our island friends helped Lee and Sheila write a thank you note in the Kapinga language. They put the message up on the bulletin boards located at each end of the central island path. The message announced that Lee would be blowing the ship's horn just before departing the next day. Lee and Sheila did not like to say good-bye and would often tell their new local friends that the world was round and they would see them later. However, this did not make things any easier, and they knew the chance of visiting this remote paradise again was very unlikely.

The next day, after making the boat ready for departure and blowing our horn, we had one last surprise. We soon noticed that almost everyone on the island had come down to the beach for a farewell send off. A large crowd had gathered to wave goodbye.

As we sailed out from the island with tears in our eyes, the islanders kept waving. They continued to watch us and wave until we were far away. Although I did not cry, my fur tingled with a feeling of love as I curled up looking back at a place I will never forget. It is definitely a place full of peace and harmony that the rest of the world could learn from.

CHAPTER 20
Budi Budi and Beyond

We were now heading south with the eventual destination of Australia. However, we would first have to sail through the southwest part of the North Pacific, pass through the Solomon Sea, and make our way through islands in the eastern part of Papua New Guinea. Then, once we entered the westernmost part of the South Pacific, there would be one final crossing over the Coral Sea to Australia. Since we were not sure where we would stop along the way, we decided to take it day by day as we came closer to the next group of islands.

Except for finding a few cockroaches that had somehow made their way onto the boat, our first few days at sea were mostly uneventful. Although we had a few equatorial rain squalls and the winds were mostly light, we made our way back south to the equator without any real problems. Once we had crossed the equator (for the third time out of seven over the years of cruising), we did encounter some bands of black clouds that brought the typical squalls and shifting winds in between periods of flat calms. Lee also noticed that the ocean currents kept changing direction. Still, nothing too dramatic happened, and we slowly made progress further south while only occasionally running the engine, which was now more dependable, since Lee had fixed the previous fuel-line problem.

During the last few days before coming close to some islands and entering the Solomon Sea, we did see a few large cargo ships.

One of them even came up very close behind us before changing course. This made Lee think of an old saying about what breaks up any boredom while sailing along in the open ocean. The proverb says that the only relief is "to see a ship or ship a sea." In case you are wondering, "to ship a sea" means that some seawater comes over the boat. Both of these occurrences will get your attention and wake you up.

However, although we did see a few other ships and avoided any collisions, what woke me up the most was a pack of dolphins that came over the horizon and surrounded the boat. They danced about for quite a while giving me wide-eyed looks. It wasn't long after this that a large school of skipjack tuna fish crossed our path, skipping over the surface of the water. Guess that's how they got their name. They definitely seemed to be in hurry. Before my mouth could even start to drool as my taste buds got excited, they were gone. Later, more dolphins came by in pursuit. That is probably why the fish did not stay long.

Not long after that, a very tired sea tern landed on the rail. This bird must have been exhausted, for he did not want to leave. The next day, I noticed he was still there. Later that day, we encountered a longer-than-usual storm squall. After things cleared, we found that the bird was no longer alive. Lee and Sheila felt sad, so they gave the bird a ritual burial at sea. I thought that was very nice of them, for I really do like birds.

When we came close to some islands near the entrance to the Solomon Sea, Lee was considering stopping at the island of Nuguria in Papua New Guinea, reported to be friendly to yachts. However, the ocean currents were erratic, and our actual position was too far to the west to make the entrance. In addition, the timing was wrong, as nighttime was now approaching. He decided it was better to head through a wide gap between some other islands and continue on south. Later, after taking another look at the charts, he decided on two possible options for stopping that were about a two-day sail away. It was just as well, for the weather had turned sour with rain and lightning, so it was not the time to search for a closer anchorage.

As we sailed on, we passed a number of local fishing boats and saw more schools of tuna prancing over the surface of the sea. Lee identified them as yellowfin tuna. Must be a good area for fishing. Lee put a line out, but had no luck. The following day, we came close to a number of floating logs, and Lee reminded me that he was happy our boat's hull was made of steel. These could easily sink a boat made of wood or fiberglass.

There were no steady trade winds blowing in this area, and the direction of the winds continued to be variable, forcing us to sometimes tack into the wind. When we considered stopping at one location, the skies became so overcast that the limited visibility made it impossible. Lee was disappointed, because he had heard that the island was full of crazy women who chased men around. It would have been interesting to see them.

While considering moving on to a more distant location, Sheila heard on the ship's radio that a cyclone was headed north off the coast of Australia. Lee then took another look at the chart and noticed a nice, small island with a good anchorage in a sheltered cove. He decided that we'd better go there and wait to see what happened with the approaching cyclone. As it turned out, it was a good decision. This remote island is part of Papua New Guinea and is called Budi Budi. It was to be the most primitive island we ever visited. It had been about seven days since we left Kapinga 630 miles back to the north, and we were eager to stop.

The small island of Budi Budi had long been a part of a group of trading islands known as the Kula Ring. The island was far from modern civilization, and the people had few possessions. The islanders used beautiful but primitive sailing canoes to sail around to these neighboring islands. In the past, they used special sea shells with carved decorations for currency, but since modern currency was hard to come by in this remote location, trading one type of product for another was their primary way of "shopping." Even though they now had some contact with the modern world, not much had changed over the centuries. We were the only yacht to come there that year, so they were happy to see us and do some trading.

The elder natives still carried on with certain old traditions, and some had facial tattoos and special large earrings that stretched out their earlobes. I could never understand why anyone would wear earrings. If I tried to put some on, my soft ears would fall down to the side of my cheeks. We also found out that these people used to be avid dancers and drummers, but sadly the arrival of the missionaries had put a stop to those practices.

The islanders lived in traditional thatched huts, but had little to put in them. One family did have a radio, but no batteries. Most of the furniture was made out of logs. Each family had small gardens with taro and other root plants, along with their share of chickens and pigs, but they lacked other basic food stuff such as rice, flour, sugar, and beans. For these items, they were dependent on the arrival of a cargo ship that rarely came their way. Since many families were poor, most of the men had gone away to find work on other islands. Besides being good divers and fishermen, those that stayed were skilled at carving and created wonderful pieces of art out of wood. They were very interested in trading their handmade carvings for better woodworking tools. Lee was happy to oblige them with some trades.

Besides making drums, walking sticks, and a variety of decorative artifacts, their woodworking skills included the carving of small dugout canoes out of logs. Each of the canoes would eventually become waterlogged, so new ones had to be repeatedly built from the local hardwood trees. Since the best trees had already been cut down, good wood was scarce, and the remaining smaller fishing canoes were very primitive, with tattered sails sewn together from pieces of cloth or flour sacks and twisted poles for masts. Each family had their own canoe, which they used for fishing in the local waters and for transportation from their nearby island homes to the small main village by the cove.

Only a few of the larger trading canoes were still in use for trading with people on more distant islands. These were actually great works of art with lots of decorative cowrie shells sewn into the woodwork. Since they had no cotton or other modern materials, their primitive sails were made of natural pandanus leaves that were stitched together. Their hulls were painted with shark oil to preserve the wood. We saw only one of these older, larger canoes sitting in storage inside a boathouse near the beach. It did not seem to be in good condition. The rest of the remaining canoes had sailed off to trade somewhere, while others had previously sunk at sea.

When we first arrived and dropped anchor, we were immediately greeted by locals in their small canoes. They quickly asked if we had any mosquito repellant. The reason for this was the presence of malaria. Even though there was an island clinic, it did little to help with the problem of this dreaded disease. Many of the inhabitants had gotten malaria more than once, and even the babies had suffered from this terrible illness. They told us that the swampy bog in the middle of the island was the cause of this problem. When sunset came, the mosquitos often moved into the village, infecting all who lived there. During the evening, many people would build a fire on a beach by a point of land, and stay there until the threat had passed. With the fire and some sea breeze on the beach, the chances of being bitten by mosquitos was reduced. However, it would still be most helpful if they had some kind of repellant. We gave them all that we could spare and made a point of not going ashore in the evening.

Even though Lee and Sheila scheduled their shore visits to the time around midday, we must have made a mistake at some

point, for after a few days at Budi Budi, Sheila started to have a fever with periods of chills and hot flashes. She did not look good. After rummaging through our medical kit, she found the appropriate pills we carried for a suspected case of malaria, and she swallowed them all. Whether or not she did have malaria, we will never know, but I am happy to say that her fever soon broke and she got better.

Besides this occurrence, most of our time at Budi Budi was quite pleasant. Each day there was a lot of trading with families that came out to our boat. Lee got some great wood carvings and had a chance to sail one of their small canoes. He also talked one of the native men into doing some drumming while visiting our boat, far from the eyes of the missionaries. Sheila gave the women gifts of clothing and served them tea and snacks. I generally kept my distance, but did get some good pats.

Although I never dared go ashore, I was entertained when I saw a nearby women throw one of her smelly pigs in the water for a bath. I am not sure how often that happens, but I guess the pig didn't mind, for he took his time swimming back to shore.

However, what was most intriguing to me was the condition of the local people's blackened teeth. I soon found out the reason for this. Many of the people living here consume a locally grown mild stimulant called betel nut. The leaves of this plant are ground up and mixed with lime into a sticky paste before being consumed. The islanders of all ages seem to like it a lot, even though the constant use of it causes their teeth to rot. I could not understand the attraction and never chewed this paste. It all seemed quite odd to me. The thought of it made me dash below to look in a mirror and see how my teeth were doing.

After staying about a week, we received a radio report that the late-season cyclone had moved away, so it was now okay for

us to continue south. Since we were getting low on certain provisions, we were anxious to arrive in Australia.

Wishing the locals well and saying goodbye, we headed out to the southern part of the Solomon Sea. I was very happy when a group of dolphins gave us an escort and pranced around the bow of the boat. Shortly after that a flock of birds, including some storm petrels passed by. I was pleased to be back at sea again, for after many years of sailing experience, I am now very much at home with the rhythm of life at sea, and even considered myself an "old salt."

We first met with light winds on our nose that kept us heading in the wrong direction, but after a while, the winds shifted and our course improved. Before long we came to an anchorage in the last group of islands in the area known as the Louisiade Archipelago. These islands form a boundary between the Solomon Sea and the Coral Sea to the south. From this location, we would set sail on a 540-mile crossing over the Coral Sea to Australia.

After spending a couple nights anchored at one small island, we set out on a course for the port of Cairns on the northeast coast of Australia. We were happy to now be back in the latitudes where the South Pacific trade winds blow.

On the first day out, Lee was surprised to catch a small shark. Although we did have some of it for dinner, it did not taste very good. Not long after that, a flying fish flew into the side of the dodger, bounced onto the stern, and fell back into the sea. It all happened very quickly, and I was glad it did not hit me in the face like the last time.

Due to the presence of a large high-pressure area in the Southern Ocean, the trade winds soon became reinforced with gusts up to thirty knots. We were now moving quite fast on a beam reach with the Aries self-steering device doing a good job of keeping the boat on course. The boat plunged across the waves and bounded along over ten-foot rolling ocean swells. Although I soon found my sea paws taking hold of the deck while my whiskers fluttered in the wind, I jumped below to a bunk where I

could relax with the constant rhythm of the boat as she pranced along.

With strong trade winds, our good ship Perelandra moved along quickly. Sheila spent much of her time on the radio talking to other cruisers, checking on any changes in the weather forecast, and getting information about the port of Cairns. With the GPS (global positioning device), Lee could keep track of our position, calculate the effect of any ocean currents, and make any corrections to the direction we sailed. With a slight adjustment to the sails, we kept our boat on the most direct heading.

Before the end of the fourth day at sea, it was "Land ho!" as we spotted land ahead. Most of the northeast coast of Australia is protected by the famous Great Barrier Reef lying a few miles offshore. However, there is a nice wide opening in the reef into the large seaport of Cairns. When we arrived in port, we soon realized we were no longer in the remote third world. We were now entering a city with all the modern conveniences. We were back in the modern world in a new country that I call the wonderful land of Oz.

During the final part of our voyage, we would have all sorts of new adventures, which will be covered in the last book of the trilogy, *Westward Over the Horizon*. There you will find more stories about the remaining two years of our global voyage as we travel on to more exotic places in the Far East, the Indian Ocean, and Africa, before crossing the Atlantic Oceans to our new home on the northeast coast of the U.S.A.

This last book of the series about our world cruise is full of amazing stories that involve encounters with aboriginals, alligators, a glowing sea, pirates, Komodo dragons, exotic religious temples, waterspouts, a boa constrictor, ugly insects, dancing elephants, spinner dolphins, coral reefs, friendly manta rays, whales, a large mahi mahi, strange jungle creatures, and dancing Zulu tribes.

In addition, there are remarkable experiences that include enduring an eight-hour lightning storm, witnessing rare native ceremonies in Madagascar, surviving our worst storm at sea, visiting an African game park, rounding the Cape of Good Hope, handling a stowaway cricket, surfing on a giant freak wave, crossing the mouth of the Amazon River, landing on Devil's Island, listening to Caribbean steel drum bands, drifting in the Atlantic doldrums, and meeting with the descendants of a famous sea cat, just to name a few.

Hope to see you there. Meow!

The Author

LeCain W. Smith, known to his friends as Captain Lee, was born near the ocean on the coast of Maine and was called to the sea early in life. Over the years, different sailboats took him on many nautical adventures, and on most every voyage, he had a cat as a companion. With time, his skills came to include teaching sailing and navigation, boat building, boat deliveries, yacht surveying, acting as a harbormaster, and chartering boats as a licensed captain. In addition, he wrote several nonfiction books with nautical, historical, and health-related themes.

While living in Port Townsend, Washington, during the 1980's, he spent five years building a forty-three-foot steel ketch and then completed a six-year voyage around the world. In company with his mate Sheila and trusted sea cat Chowder, this extensive exploration took them through many remote islands of paradise and exotic parts of the world.

When it was over, Chowder felt that all their adventures were definitely worth sharing. Since Captain Lee had produced *Far Away*, a documentary video about the South Pacific part of their voyage, Chowder decided to tell her own version of the complete story in a trilogy of books—*Sailing South 'til the Butter Melts, Far Away Islands of Paradise,* and *Westward Beyond the Horizon.*

CPSIA information can be obtained
at www.ICGtesting.com
Printed in the USA
JSHW032339210222
23160JS00002B/3

9 780961 550868